GOD AND THE GIFT
An Ecumenical Theology of Giving

Risto Saarinen

LITURGICAL PRESS
Collegeville, Minnesota

www.litpress.org

A title of the Unitas Books series published by the Liturgical Press

Other titles available in the Unitas Books series:

Justification and the Future of the Ecumenical Movement:
The Joint Declaration on the Doctrine of Justification
  William G. Rusch, ed.

I Believe, Despite Everything: Reflections of an Ecumenist
  Jean-Marie R. Tillard

Visible Church, Visible Unity: Ecumenical Ecclesiology and
"The Great Tradition of the Church"
  Ola Tjørhom

Communio Sanctorum: The Church as the Communion of Saints
  Official German Catholic–Lutheran Dialogue

One with God: Salvation as Deification and Justification
  Veli-Matti Kärkkäinen

Cover design by Keith McCormick

1   2   3   4   5   6   7   8

Library of Congress Cataloging-in-Publication Data

Saarinen, Risto.
    God and the gift : an ecumenical theology of giving / Risto Saarinen.
       p. cm. — (Unitas books)
    Includes bibliographical references and index.
    ISBN 13: 978-0-8146-3013-6 (pbk. : alk. paper)
    ISBN 10: 0-8146-3013-8
    1. Gifts—Religious aspects—Christianity. 2. Theology. I. Title. II. Series.

  BR115.G54S23 2004
  231.7—dc22   2004019559

Unitas Books

On the eve of his crucifixion, Jesus prayed that his followers "may all be one" (John 17:21). Christians believe that this promise is fulfilled in the Church. The Church is Christ's body, and his body cannot be divided. And yet, the churches today live in contradiction to that promise. Churches that recognize in another Christian community an embodiment of the one Church of Jesus Christ still too often find that they cannot live in true communion with them. This contradiction between the Church's unity and its division has driven the ecumenical movement over the last century.

The pursuit of unity will require more than a few mutual adjustments among the Churches. Ecumenism must involve true conversion, a conversion both of hearts and minds, of the will and the intellect. We all must learn to think in new ways about the teachings and practices of the Church. Division has become deeply embedded in the everyday life and thought of the churches. Thinking beyond division will require a new outlook.

Unitas Books seeks to serve the rethinking that is a necessary part of the ecumenical movement. Some books in the series will directly address important topics of ecumenical discussion; others will chart and analyze the ecumenical movement itself. All will be concerned with the Church's unity. Their authors will be ecumenical experts from a variety of Christian traditions, but the books will be written for a wider audience of interested clergy and laypersons. We hope they will be informative for the expert and the newcomer alike.

The unity we seek will be a gift of the Holy Spirit. The Spirit works through means, however, and one of the Spirit's means is careful theological reflection and articulate communication. We hope that this series may be used by the Spirit so that the unity won by Christ may be more fully visible "so that the world may believe" (John 17:21).

Norman A. Hjelm
Michael Root
William G. Rusch

The series editor responsible for this volume is Michael Root.

Contents

Acknowledgments

It was the Finnish Luther scholar Tuomo Mannermaa who first turned my attention to the theological notion of the gift. A characterization of salvation as gift preserves the ontological reality of the gospel message without becoming philosophical or materialistic; it also underlines the social dimension of faith without reducing it to sociology. In my work with the ecumenical dialogues of the Lutheran World Federation since the early 1990s, I have often been fascinated by the many theological, philosophical, and social connotations that various Christian churches ascribe to the ideas of gift and giving.

Although the background of this book can be found both in Luther studies and in ecumenism, the study is neither historical nor does it attempt at outlining another ecumenical ecclesiology. It is rather a systematic discussion of some prominent theological features attached to giving and the gift. Of course, I hope that this discussion can be relevant for both ecumenism and the academic treatment of gift.

I have tested my thoughts with many audiences: in the postgraduate seminar on "Grace and Gift" at Yale Divinity School, October 2002; in the meeting "The Future of Lutheran Theology" at Aarhus University, Denmark, January 2003; at the Castelli Colloquium on "Gift and Debt" at the University of Rome, January 2004; and on various occasions at the University of Helsinki. My thanks are due to all who have commented my interpretations, especially to Gil Bailie, Bo Kristian Holm, Sammeli Juntunen, Simo Knuuttila, and Miroslav Volf. I have also greatly benefited of the discussions with a group of my Helsinki students who read and commented the whole manuscript during Spring 2004.

A very special thanks is due to Michael Root who has again re-vised my language and, as an editor of Unitas Books, very effectively taken care of the relations with the Liturgical Press.

Helsinki, July 2004, Risto Saarinen

Introduction: Giving and Receiving

Giving and receiving are basic human actions. In religious life, giving can also be portrayed as divine action. God is the supreme giver, whereas human persons remain receivers. Human beings give gifts and commodities to their neighbors, but sometimes theologians have said that humans cannot give anything to God. Does this mean that God can only be a giver, not a receiver? This issue is complex, since there are special modes of giving in which the gift or token is not material, but a mental or linguistic reality. Thanksgiving, for instance, is a mode of giving in which the traditional language of liturgy speaks of us giving something to God. Prayer, promise, and sacrifice may also be human activities in which God receives something from us.

The language of giving and receiving is prominent in many contemporary ecumenical agreements and doctrinal texts of the churches. Ecumenism is often explained in terms of an "exchange of gifts" among the churches. One starting-point for this terminology is the Dogmatic Constitution on the Church, *Lumen gentium*, of the Second Vatican Council. *Lumen gentium* speaks of each individual part of the universal church contributing through its special gifts to the good of the other parts and of the whole church. In one sense this gift exchange among the people of God is horizontal, from humans to humans. But *Lumen gentium* also says that the character of universality present in this exchange is "a gift from the Lord."[1]

---

[1] See *Lumen gentium*, 13, in *Vatican Council II, The Conciliar and Post Conciliar Documents*, ed., Austin Flannery, O.P. (Boston: St. Paul Editions 1988) here: 364–65. For language of gift exchange, see Margaret O'Gara, *The Ecumenical Gift Exchange* (Collegeville: Liturgical Press, 1998).

In this way it is common in theology and ecumenism to say that the vertical gift from God to humans is a prerequisite of horizontal sharing among human beings. God's vertical gift creates and sustains the unity and catholicity present in the manifold field of human charisms which are extended horizontally. *Lumen gentium* here characterizes this reality of sharing among the people of God as "fullness in unity" and as "catholic unity." An adequate conceptualization of divine and human giving is needed in order to understand properly this intimate relationship among divine gift, human sharing, unity, and catholicity.

In its statements on unity, the World Council of Churches has likewise adopted the language of giving gifts. The unity statement of New Delhi assembly (1961) speaks of "the unity which is both God's will and his gift to his Church." The title of the WCC Canberra unity statement (1991) reads: *The Unity of the Church as Koinonia: Gift and Calling*. According to the Canberra statement, the church shares in the grace of Jesus Christ, the love of God, and the communion of the Holy Spirit. These gifts enable the church to be a servant of reconciliation. In this calling, the church provides healing and aims at overcoming various divisions. The structure of "gift and calling," often repeated in the documents of the ecumenical movement, serves the purpose of showing how the human struggle for unity, reconciliation, and healing is a fruit of the vertical gift coming from God.[2]

The Perspective of Reception

Both in the Catholic church and in the World Council of Churches, ecumenical work is thus presented in terms of giving. On a closer look, however, a student of ecumenical texts is surprised to realize how little the concept of giving has been elaborated by theologians and ecumenists. The interest of ecumenical theologians has clearly concentrated on the other end of this act, namely on receiving. At least since Yves Congar's famous study on "reception" as ecclesial reality, the issue of receiving new truths in the church has been in the focus of ec-

---

[2] The texts are available, e.g., in *The Ecumenical Movement: An Anthology of Key Texts and Voices*, ed. Michael Kinnamon and Brian E. Cope (Geneva: World Council of Churches, 1997). For the relevance of New Delhi today, see *In One Body through the Cross: The Princeton Proposal for Christian Unity*, eds. Carl Braaten and Robert Jenson (Grand Rapids: Eerdmans, 2003).

umenists. André Birmelé's recent overview of the ecumenical discussion since Congar shows the many sides of the issue of reception.[3]

Congar describes reception as a process through which a church integrates into its life and thought a new truth which it did not have previously, but which the church after a process of deliberation finds plausible and compatible with the earlier truths. Birmelé points out that this kind of reception cannot limit itself to a merely administrative decision. The new truth must in some way become known and begin to permeate the concrete life of the church. It is this appropriation and practical influence that enables us to say that the doctrinal formulations of the ecumenical councils are received in the church. Or, as in the case of the council of Florence 1439, the lack of reception shows that an administrative decision alone cannot change the life of the church.

The activity of ecumenical reception, emphasized by Congar, Birmelé, and many others, is instructive in that it shows how a true reception is not a passive state, but on closer inspection becomes, and should become, a process of giving and transmitting the gifts received. The very process of giving gifts to others through time and space becomes a criterion of genuine reception. Receiving becomes defined in terms of giving. Furthermore, reception is never finished. According to Birmelé, a received truth or "gift" must always be re-received, to be learnt and put into practice again in order not to be forgotten. The elements of repetition and circulation begin to show themselves. Birmelé compares ecclesial reception to a theater piece: the same piece is adapted very differently on different stages, but we can still recognize that it is the same piece.[4] It is thus a non-identical repetition which characterizes reception.

So we see that although the issue of giving is not explicitly and thematically treated by ecumenists, the underlying dynamics of giving and the circulation of gifts becomes evident when reception is studied. Reception is not a passive hearing or reading, but the recipients must live, repeat, and circulate the truth they have received. Reception put into practice becomes giving. There is a connection of reciprocity between giving and receiving in the issue of ecumenical reception, a connection which will be more closely studied in the course of this book. But, clearly, the explicit preference of the ecumenists has been on the

[3] For the following, see Yves Congar, "La reception comme réalité ecclesiologique," *Revue des sciences philosophiques et théologiques* 1972, 369–403; André Birmelé, *La communion ecclésiale: Progrès oecuméniques et enjeux methodologiques* (Paris: Cerf, 2000) esp. 361–89.

[4] Birmelé 2000, 363, 367.

side of "receiving." The side of giving is a sub-structure that only becomes visible when the phenomenon of receiving is elaborated.

Ecumenical reception concerns churches and communities of faith. There is an obvious analogy to the individual person's receiving new religious truths. This individual phenomenon is many-sided, since it concerns religious education as well as conversion and new commitments in new life situations. At this stage I will only point at the classical issue of Pelagianism in Western theology, that is, the issue in which sense we receive grace with our free will. Both Catholics and Protestant reject historical Pelagianism, or the teaching that the free will plays a major role in the reception of grace. But there are various differences in how theology copes with human freedom after the rejection of Pelagianism. The alleged passivity of the human receiver is a major theme of Catholic theology at least since Augustine and of Protestant theology since its Lutheran beginnings.

We cannot here enter into the details of this discussion but will only make two preliminary remarks which connect the topic with the overall theme of this book. First, this "receiver-oriented" view of post-Augustinian theology is a rather Western or Latin phenomenon that is not shared by the Orthodox churches. Eastern Orthodoxy normally claims that there is a synergy, a cooperation between God and the human person in salvation. This claim is not made in order to build an anthropocentric theology. On the contrary, Orthodox theology seeks to say that God is not saving a stone or a bookshelf. God is saving persons, and persons are characterized by their ability to respond to God's giving act, the salvific act in the sacraments. Human "free will" is thus seen from a giver-oriented perspective, and this perspective allows the claim of synergy without consideration of the Pelagian controversy. Somewhat paradoxically, the giver-oriented view goes together with the affirmation of synergy. Through employing a theocentric or a giver-oriented perspective, Orthodox theologians can avoid many classical controversies of Western theology.

Second, the self-limitation of theology to the details of human reception is not only Western but also in many ways modern. At least since Immanuel Kant, but perhaps already since the introduction into Latin of Aristotle in the thirteenth century, Western philosophy and theology has been occupied by a search for the pre-conditions and "transcendental" limits of human knowledge. According to this paradigm, we receive everything through our senses and our knowledge is fundamentally pre-conditioned by the very process of receiving. Critical philosophy and academic theology thus almost necessarily become not only receiver-oriented but receiver-centered, since the conditions of the recipient determine the nature of our knowledge and language.

In Western theology, the anti-Pelagian attitude has often been expressed by 1 Corinthians 4:7b: "What do you have that you did not receive?"[5] This verse can be looked at from a receiver-oriented perspective. Then one must think about the freedom pertaining to the reception and construct a human person who is not free but who nevertheless has a certain freedom of consenting to the issue at hand. But 1 Corinthians 4:7 works probably in a more adequate manner if it is looked at from a giver-oriented perspective. Then the sentence points to the Giver who is responsible for all: for creation, salvation, and the final destiny. It is not human freedom that is at stake, but God's overflowing goodness and activity in giving everything as gift. Of course, the giver-oriented reading does not solve the philosophical issue of human free will. But it enables the reader to see God's grace in terms of divine giving rather than in terms of a definition of human possibilities.

In Protestant theology, we can identify similar currents which counteract the dominance of post-Enlightenment epistemological and anthropocentric perspectives. Karl Barth's theological program is an especially prominent case. Barth refuses to treat theology in terms of anthropological preconditions and concentrates on God's self-revelation. In this way he creates a giver's perspective from which theology can be laid out. The appeal of Barthianism and many other "post-liberal" theologies, for instance of Robert Jenson,[6] lies in their ability to speak of God's self-revelation and self-giving. They are developing a different optic that enables us to speak of God in terms of giving, thus counteracting the Enlightenment perspective of human preconditions.

In keeping with these examples, it will be argued in this book that we may gain something through looking at ecumenically decisive doctrinal issues from the perspective of the giver. Let it be said at once that this cannot take place in a naïve fashion. We are conditioned by the fact that we are humans and thus discuss the issue of giving from the viewpoint of human understanding and human language. When we speak of the Giver, the divine actor, we are doing so by transcending our

---

[5] I am here employing the instructive discussion in David Berger, *Natur und Gnade* (Regensburg: Roderer, 1998) here: 426.

[6] Jenson has elaborated divine giving in "Triune Grace," *dialog* 41 (2002) 285–93.

human knowledge and language in a manner which is to some extent metaphorical. We must reflect the contemporary discussion on gifts and giving precisely in order to be aware of this metaphorical nature of divine giving.

The issue is rather complex, since even when we speak of other human beings giving us something, we perform a small act of faith. Strictly speaking, we do not know the intentions of other people, the givers whose minds we cannot read. Is my neighbor giving me this thing as a gift, or should we rather speak of mutual commitments, economic exchange and entering into contract? A small act of faith is needed when a gift is believed to be a free gift.

We will devote the second chapter of this book to the attempt to read some well-known theological texts from the perspective of giving rather than receiving. It will be argued throughout the book that the dominant perspective of human reception, although as such fully adequate, has prohibited us from seeing the other side of the coin, namely, the giving that occurs in the process of receiving. In this sense a giver-oriented perspective may provide an added value to many issues.

If the great discussion topic of ecumenical theology of the last decades has been reception, one of the great themes of contemporary philosophical theology has been "the gift." As will be shown in more detail in chapter 1, recent work by Jacques Derrida, Jean-Luc Marion, and others has brought the gift to the focus of academic theology and philosophy of religion. One reason behind this new interest in the gift is the claim of sociologists and anthropologists that there simply cannot be anything like a "free gift." All gifts are conditioned by some self-interest of the giver. This claim presents a challenge to our classical view of God's free gifts.

The classical idea does not only come from theology. Already Aristotle described the gift as "something given without recompense" (*Topics* 125a18). Anthropology thus challenges classical philosophy as well. On the other hand, the prominence of "free gifts" both in theology and in everyday life also presents a challenge to the sociological claim.

How do we conceive God in the context of this contemporary discussion? My preliminary hypothesis is that the discussion can be fruitfully shifted from the product, that is, the gift, to the productive act, that is, the basic act of giving. A conceptual analysis of the act of giving may shed some new light on the philosophical discussion concerning gifts. An ecumenist certainly must be modest in claiming that he could contribute something in the field of philosophical theology. But an ecumenist cannot afford to be superficial or naive when claiming something regarding the complex issue of "gift exchange." It is astonishing that, forty years after *Lumen gentium* and the World Council of Churches' New Delhi unity statement, ecumenists have hardly taken notice of the extensive contemporary discussions of "gift exchange." This book will be a modest attempt to take at least some notice and to overcome the accusation that ecumenists do not contribute to the wider theological discussion.

"The gift" is not only a prominent subject of academic discussion, but also, and more importantly, a central interpretative notion in the theological self-understanding of the Christian churches. As we saw from *Lumen gentium*, the divine gift establishes and preserves unity and catholicity among Christians, but in a way this is only a secondary use of the divine gift. First and foremost, the divine gift is a gift of salvation, a gift of faith, a gift of grace given in and through baptism and the Eucharist. This is the primary use of the term "gift," for instance, in the Lutheran–Roman Catholic *Joint Declaration on the Doctrine of Justification*.

In this ecumenical document, Catholics and Lutherans declare together that they share the same basic truths regarding salvation as the justification of sinners. Both confession teach that in baptism, sinners "are granted the gift of salvation." The churches also in this context speak of "the free gift of faith" which justifies the human person. God further "imparts the gift of new life in Christ."[7] In all these expressions, the language of gift underlines the sovereign role of God as Giver and downplays human activity. The salvific gift in all its dimensions remains unconditioned in the sense that it is not made dependent of human merits or activities.

A philosopher or sociologist might here ask whether such free gifts are at all conceivable. A systematic theologian will see that although the explicit emphasis of this text is on the gift, the implicit issue is nevertheless human reception and human response. Since Augustine and certainly since Luther, the doctrine of grace and salvation is massively concerned with the possibilities of human achievement and merit in responding to grace. Therefore, it is not so much the gift as gift but the gift as opposed to merit which is at stake in the discussion between Catholics and Lutherans. "The free gift of faith" does not focus

---

[7] Joint Declaration on the Doctrine of Justification, 1999, § 22, 25, in: *Growth in Agreement vol. 2*, ed. Harding Meyer et al. (Grand Rapids: Eerdmans, 2000) 569–70.

on God's intentions, but it attempts to rule out the false alternative of faith as human accomplishment. Such a "receiver-oriented approach" to the issue of justification, however, makes the gift appear in a peculiar light. A "giver-oriented" perspective may correct the one-sided Western understanding of the gift of salvation.

Our Task

The starting-point of this book lies in the observation that contemporary ecumenical, theological, and philosophical discussions center around the issues of reception and the gift but neglect the basic act of giving. In view of this observation it is asked: can we approach these discussions from the perspective of giver and from the very act of giving? If so, what will these discussions look like?

It will be argued that we do have theological resources that enable us to outline a "theology of giving." They provide an opportunity to approach old problems from a relatively new viewpoint. As already indicated, chapters 1 and 2 will deal with basic philosophical and theological resources. After this, we will outline some specific modes of giving, in particular forgiveness (ch. 3), sacrifice and thanksgiving (ch. 4), and imitation or "giving an example" (ch. 5).

The present book has three different but related aims.

(i) It attempts to outline a brief theology of giving. For this purpose, it employs both classical theology and contemporary discussions.

(ii) This study also points out the ecumenical relevance of the theology of giving. It will be argued that many traditional ecumenical problems can be approached from a fresh perspective which yields some new and unexpected results. Especially the last chapter (ch. 6) is devoted to this aim.

(iii) For those who are more interested in particular theological and philosophical topics, some new interpretations will be offered for further discussion. Among these are an interpretation of forgiveness as "negative giving" (ch. 3), a discussion of the relationship between sacrifice and divine non-violence (ch. 4) and a new proposal to conceptualize various types of Christian imitation (ch. 5).

These aims are connected with our overall claim that instead of looking at reception and the gift we should focus on the issue of giving. We can already here illustrate this shift of perspective with some observations and examples. Our examples will not be discussed exhaustively, but they serve as preliminary signposts showing us the way to proceed.

Since giving and receiving are basic acts, the words denoting those acts have a roughly similar basic meaning and often parallel pragmatic uses in different languages. One semantic feature of the verb "to give" is that both the giver and the receiver are normally supposed to be persons or at least living beings. If the receiver is not a person, we use some other verb, for instance: I give this book to you, but: I put this book on the bookshelf. We may grant that there are all kinds of metaphorical and auxiliary uses of the verb "to give," for instance "giving up," "giving birth to an idea," *es gibt* (German: there is) or *cette chambre donne sur le jardin* (French: this room has a view of, or "gives onto," the garden), but the basic rule is obvious: we give to other people.

Animals and plants are an interesting case in this respect, since we give food to dogs and even give water to plants. In these examples, the receiver is expected to respond or react in some way. But if our action does not provoke any response, other verbs are preferred in dealing with animals and plants.

The semantic rules of giving gifts are similar, perhaps even stricter in the sense that the receiver must be a person. If somebody is giving gifts to his or her pets, we think that this human giver has personified the animal in question. In most cases we do not speak of giving gifts to animals or plants, and there is certainly no point in saying that this gift is given to a particular stone or bookshelf.

We noticed above that the receiver-oriented view of theological gifts is, at least in anti-Pelagian contexts, employed in order to downplay the receiver's activity. Now we find, however, that the giver-oriented optic yields a different result: giving a gift, and perhaps giving in general, only makes sense when the receiver is in some way active. In order to speak of giving and gifts we must normally assume a response or reaction from the receiver. This observation is very simple, but it may puzzle a religious person who is accustomed to speak of gifts only as opposed to the receiver's merits or cooperation.

One proposal to solve this puzzle could be to say that we use the words "give" and "gift" differently in theological contexts. But this proposal does not hold, as the following example of infant baptism shows. The churches practicing infant baptism normally emphasize the fundamental importance of baptism as gift. A recent Lutheran statement on baptism characterizes this as follows: "Baptism as sacrament points to its fundamental character as gift and as the medium by which gifts are given. In baptism, we are receivers. . . . The fundamentally receptive character is evident in its liturgical form. One cannot baptize oneself. Baptism must be received from another person. . . . The gift character of baptism is also evident in the simplicity, even ease, of baptism. At the crucial moment, all one need do is be quiet and be still . . . Baptism requires no prior physical, intellectual, moral, or religious attainments."[8]

This typical receiver-oriented view of baptism downplays all human activity in receiving the theological gift. But the case of baptism is more complex. Let us imagine a strict Lutheran who supports infant baptism, denies all salvific cooperation between God and humans and says that salvation is entirely a free gift of God. This Lutheran is "monergistic": he believes that God alone effects the salvation of the infant to be baptized.

Given that God alone brings about the change, a complete outsider hearing this argumentation might think that one could baptize stones, bookshelves, and dead persons, since "nothing" is required of the receiver. But every Christian knows that this is not true. Even the most consistently monergistic Protestant thinks that the means of grace can only be administered to living persons. Thus they think that the recipient must in some genuine sense be a recipient, in other words, that giving is only meaningful when there is active receiving.

Thus there is a difference between monergism and automatism. Even when a theological gift is given in a monergistic fashion, the receivers must meet certain requirements. These requirements do not refer to their activities, but to their being. The requirement to be a living person corresponds to the regular semantics of "giving" described above, and thus in theology the theological gift is spoken of in a way which is similar to other gifts.

Especially in many variants of Protestant theology, "faith" refers to a condition that is not an active deed, but is nevertheless required in order that the gift of salvation be actual. The notion of faith thus serves the purpose of distinguishing between monergism and automatism. The Lutheran Confessions, for instance, condemn the view that the sacraments work automatically or *ex opere operato* (Latin: by the mere performance of an act). This condemnation was launched in order to fight the view that the Mass automatically blots out the sins of both the living and

---

[8] *Baptism and the Unity of the Church*, eds. Michael Root and Risto Saarinen (Grand Rapids: Eerdmans, 1998) 18.

the dead. Given such a view, one Mass could be said for many persons and thus an industry of saying Masses could develop with the purpose of providing automatic forgiveness even for absent and dead people.[9]

In order to stop this automatism, the Lutheran Reformation insisted that a personal reception of the sacrament in faith was necessary. It is important to see that this decision has nothing to do with anthropocentrism or subjectivism. It is not faith which creates or performs the sacrament. A giver-oriented optic is here at stake, saying that the sacrament is a gift of God, from God, and in fact the sacrament is God himself present in, with, and under the bread and wine. But in order that this objective act can be an act of giving, and not merely a movement at the altar, there must be a living and faithful recipient present at the occasion. In this context of discussion, faith does not signalize a cooperative act, but a personal participation in the reciprocity of giving and receiving. A gift cannot be given if the receiver is not there.

Thus in theology, too, gifts go together with the requirement of a reception of the gifts. An item that is put somewhere cannot automatically transform itself into a gift. It must be received by a person in order to be a gift. The recipient need not do anything, but certain requirements need nevertheless to be met. At least four requirements can be read from the Lutheran Confessions: (1) that the recipient is alive, (2) is faithful, (3) is a person and (4) is not just anybody, a placeholder or a representative of a larger group, but the very person to whom the sacrament is physically given. In order to see this necessary differentiation of a doctrinal issue, a "giver-oriented" optic is useful.

Infant baptism is perhaps the classic example of the existence of such receptive requirements. On the one hand, the baby is doing nothing. On the other hand, the gift can only be given to a living recipient who is a person. The theological gift thus requires a certain openness for which only a living personal receiver is capable. This means that there is not a specific grammar of faith concerning gifts. We speak of giving gifts in theology in a manner which is basically similar to the regular everyday idiom. At this stage we can therefore say that the requirements of non-theological giving and receiving are more or less the same as outlined by these theological examples. In the second chapter we will refine the philosophical discussion concerning giving among human persons.

[9] See e.g. Augsburg Confession, 24, in *The Book of Concord, The Confessions of the Evangelical Lutheran Church*, eds., Robert Kolb and Timothy Wengert (Minneapolis: Fortress, 2000) 69–71, 260–69.

Baptism and the concept of faith are theological examples that show us how the notions of giving and gift can differentiate doctrinal meanings. Let us yet look, as the last introductory remark of this first chapter, at one more issue pertaining to the differentiation of meanings with the help of giver-oriented vs. receiver-oriented perspectives. This last set of illustrations is concerned with the analogies between giving and receiving on the one hand and the issue of communication on the other. In both, a basically three-place relation is at stake.

For communication, a (1) sender, a (2) message and a (3) receiver are required, and these three roughly correspond to the (1) giver, the (2) gift, and the (3) recipient. The three elements are necessary but by no means sufficient when the phenomenon of giving or the event of communication is characterized. Communication occurs in a (4) certain context, a medium or media. Giving and receiving also normally require a specific context in order to be understood. Giving bread at the communion table differs from giving it at the kitchen table. In addition, both communication and giving gifts normally occur for some (5) purpose that the participants should to be aware of. This purpose is distinct from the receiver: a ransom or a payment, for instance, can be given for my sake, although I am not the receiver of this act. The same act of gift-giving may look dramatically different when the different aims are revealed. A gift may become a bribe or a sacrifice, depending on the purpose for which it is given. Analogically, the same piece of news may serve very different purposes.

The emphases and preferences of communication also display certain similarities with our topic. Communication can be sender-oriented or receiver-oriented; it can be unilateral or dialogical. At first glance, one-way communication resembles the phenomenon of giving gifts, whereas a dialogical communication resembles gift exchange or economic exchange. On closer inspection, however, things become more complex, since unilateral communication and unilateral giving do not make much sense if the receiver does not respond. But if the receiver responds, the communication becomes dialogical, and the event of giving gifts becomes a reciprocal exchange.

In his study on the history of the idea of communication, John Durham Peters[10] has paid attention to these analogies and their theoretical and even theological significance. Communication is related to

---

[10] For the following, cf. John Durham Peters, *Speaking into the Air: A History of the Idea of Communication* (Chicago: The University of Chicago Press, 1999) esp. 3–10, 43–62.

gifts and giving already etymologically, since the notion stems from the Latin word *munus* which can mean a gift or a public duty. Gifts and duties are in a sense unilateral, since they clearly distinguish between the giver and the receiver of the *munus*. Peters points out that the English word "communication" has preserved this unilateral meaning in some old-fashioned contexts. Thus we can still speak of an academic publication as scientific communication, or of a Catholic Christian who communicates by consuming bread and wine in the Eucharist. In the first example, the publication as a medium of unilateral communication is highlighted, in the second, the one-way communication is the act of the receiver.

Clearly, in the primary contemporary use of "communication," we nevertheless think of its reciprocal and dialogical character, alluded to by the Latin word *communio*. Peters wants to affirm both the unilateral and the reciprocal meanings. He organizes them into two basic patterns, both of which are classical. The dialogical paradigm is labeled the model of Socrates, who in Plato's writings approaches the truth by means of dialogue and interactive counseling. The dissemination or *munus* paradigm is for Peters the model of Jesus, since in the parable of the sower the seed is distributed unilaterally everywhere without interaction or even regard to whether the soil is fertile or not.

At first, there seems to be a difference of value between the two models: whereas the one-way dissemination paradigm is authoritarian, wasteful, and ineffective, the dialogical and reciprocal communication appears as inherently democratic, economic, and effective: if a community can freely discuss a topic, it can perhaps achieve a rational consensus which approaches the truth.

Applying the ideas of Peters, we may argue, however, that in reality things are much more complex. The advantage of modifying communication with the help of interaction has its price. First, the message may lose something of its original integrity and authenticity when it becomes modified in the process of exchange. Second, the sender's possibility of controlling the message may be a disadvantage. In Plato, Socrates is not participating in an authority-free discussion, but he behaves like a doctor or therapist who gives advice to patients. As a therapist he has an authority over the pupils. If in this kind of therapeutic dialogue the sender is initially wrong, he nevertheless has the possibility of conjectures and new pretexts when the pupil or the group reacts. Thus a wrong opinion does not die out, but continues its existence in a modified fashion.

Third, one-way communication may be better than its reputation. Advertising, for instance, is only rarely done in an interactive fashion. An announcement or a broadcasting of the message is regarded to be simple and effective communication by the advertisers. The dissemination model is also democratic in the sense that the message is public and open to discussion and falsification. A dialogical message easily remains esoteric, since it is confined to a small group of insiders. In the parable of the sower, the seed is a very democratic and public gift to everybody. The sender cannot control this gift after its dissemination. Thus the receiver in a certain sense has more freedom with the message than in the Socratic model.

This elaboration of the models of communication shows in what senses both the unilateral act of giving or sending and the process of dialogical exchange can be either advantageous or disadvantageous in their specific contexts. When we come to the final rounds of the game of communication, we note a partial merger of Socratic and Jesuanic models. There probably is no one-way communication in the strict sense, since an advertiser or a broadcaster is aiming at some kind of reaction. And there probably is no such dialogue in which the participants would be identical in all respects.

In these final rounds of communication, it is the interplay of self and other that is at stake. The dissemination paradigm has an inherent tendency to emphasize the others, that is, the message and the receivers. We do not know much of the sower, but we know from the parable that the seed is good and that there are diverse recipients. The dialogue paradigm may in its worst form become a constrained and unfruitful occupation with the self or with the few insiders. It is the balance between self and others that is essential for good communication.

1

The Gift: Contemporary Approaches

During my childhood our family always spent the summer months in a cottage in the Finnish countryside. My father, a schoolteacher in Helsinki, originated from that area and knew well the farmers of the village. For the farmers, the summer months were a period of intensive and collective work, a time spent in making hay for the cows, growing and harvesting vegetables. Among the rural people, mutual voluntary help was necessary in order that all work could be accomplished in due time. It was essential to keep good social relations with your neighbors, since you could then count on their help in harvest time.

Summer visitors from Helsinki did not automatically belong to this network of labor exchange. But if they were relatives or wanted to keep good contact with the farmers, their help was very welcome. The big problem was, however, that the locals could not pay for this help. Neither side would give or take money, and the summer visitors had no need for the farmers' labor. The farmers were keen on rewarding all help they had received, perhaps in part for reasons of fairness and honor, but also for the simple reason that they wanted to secure the same help during the next year's harvesting season.

This was precisely what the people on holiday, including my parents, wanted to avoid. They would help the farmers out of generosity and the need for exercise, but they did not want to feel committed to this rather heavy and time-consuming labor every summer. The problem was actualized when the farmers started to give gifts to the summer visitors who had been helping them. The gift was carefully masked not to look like a return for the work accomplished, a payment or a commodity involving some kind of contract for the future. It was normally a farewell present at the end of the summer, or sometimes a Christmas present, given emphatically as a free gift.

One Christmas our family received a rather expensive and particularly ugly glass plate as gift from a neighborhood farmer. It was colorful and shaped like a fish, not a piece for urban taste. My parents were troubled since they rightly interpreted the meaning of this gift to be that they would have to spend a good deal of next year's holiday in hard farm work. But my little brother, who did not yet understand the social contract underlying the gift, was puzzled. Why should someone be troubled for receiving such a lucrative plate as a free gift?

This story shows some ambivalences in the phenomenon of giving gifts. Gifts are given in order to enhance the social role of the giver and to impose an obligation on the receiver. In the story it is not only the ugly glass plate that imposes the obligation. The first problem emerges when the summer visitors offer their help to the farmers "for free." This puts the farmer into a debt which is both a debt of gratitude and, more importantly, a debt with regard to next year's need for labor, given that the same amount of work is needed every year. The debt cannot be compensated by money or by the farmer's own labor, and therefore a gift is used to even the accounts.

Neither the giver nor the receiver can, however, say explicitly that this is how the system works. They must both behave as if each in turn gives and receives free gifts that involve no commitment and are not payments of any kind. The illusion of free gift is a necessary part of hospitality among the participants of this exchange. From my little brother's perspective, this illusion was the whole story. But from the adult perspective, the gift exchange was a subtle way of imposing commitments.

The circle of exchange is here more important than the way it originally started. My parents probably repented their initial goodwill and generosity that prompted them to offer help in the first year of harvesting. But perhaps they needed some service from the farmer that year, and the proper way of creating trust was to offer help during the harvesting season. Groups of persons are often tied to other groups with such invisible liaisons, and perhaps nobody remembers anymore how the liaison of mutual services originated. But, as a result of such liaisons, our attics become filled with gifts we did not want in the first place.

The story can be interpreted in terms of good manners and proper tactics in dealing with other people. Contemporary anthropologists, sociologists, and philosophers have, however, paid increasing attention to the theoretical issues of gifts and giving. They claim that something more fundamental and more interesting than good manners is at stake in the phenomenon of giving and receiving gifts. Giving and receiving reflect basic structures of our societies. They may even cast light on the philosophical issues concerning language and knowledge. Many philosophers of religion claim that gifts and giving are fundamentally important for theology as well. For these reasons, it is important to outline some contemporary interpretations and claims (ch. 1), before we can proceed to a more general presentation of what classical theology has said about giving and gifts (ch. 2).

From Mauss to Bourdieu

Marcel Mauss's *The Gift*[1] is generally regarded to be the starting-point of contemporary discussion on gifts. Analyzing the institution of the *potlatch*, for example, a feast among Northwest native Americans, to which every person in turn invites their neighbors and competes with them in offering hospitality, Mauss shows how complex social rules guide the gift-giving practices. Although the gifts in mutual hospitality appear, and are meant to appear, free and disinterested, they are in fact highly interested.

Even before the use of money, societies had a sort of market economy. Mauss argues that this economy was based on the mutual exchange of gifts. The social obligation of exchanging gifts provided the archaic societies with a possibility of acquiring goods and obtaining social services when needed. Through this exchange, a social and economic hierarchy was established. The ability to give to those in need increases one's social status. The drive for social status leads to competition through lavish expenditures. Giving abundant gifts for the sake of competitive status can be destructive for individuals and cause instability in the society as a whole. The circle of gift-giving may be a vicious circle.

In the story told above, the vicious circle was started by the summer visitors who helped the farmers for free. Thus they increased their

---

[1] The French original *Essai sur le don*, appeared in 1924. In the following I summarize Mauss' argument, following the English edition *Essay on the Gift* (London: Routledge, 1990). This edition includes Mary Douglas's preface "No Free Gifts."

own social standing and obligated the farmer to lift his status by donating the glass plate in return. As a result, my parents felt the need to
work even harder next summer. In Mauss's examples, such stories of
competition escalate into violence, warfare, and sinking one's own
property voluntarily into the sea.

In this sense the institution of giving gifts is interested, not "free."
At the same time, gift-giving is not utilitarian in any strict sense but
often leads, motivated by competition, to conscious waste. The institution of gifts was perhaps the first form of market economy, but gift exchange was and is nevertheless different from the utilitarian economy
of buying and selling goods. The giver of a gift is interested in getting
a better social status and an insurance or social security in the case he
or she might need help. But this is not done as a utilitarian investment.
The need of lavish expenditures for the sake of status and the vicious
circles involved in always returning more than one has received show
in what ways archaic gift exchange differs from utilitarian rationalism.

In spite of this anti-utilitarian trait, the main lesson the anthropologists learned from Mauss was that there is no free gift. If somebody offers you a gift, this person is increasing his or her social status and
putting you in his or her debt. It belongs to the idea of gift that this is
not said but, on the contrary, explicitly denied. But in reality there are
no free gifts, as Mary Douglas emphasizes in her preface to the English
edition (1990) of Mauss's essay. The whole society can be described
through monitoring the circulation of exchanges which creates the duties and social obligations of its members. In this way Mauss's book
undermined Aristotle's view of the gift as "something given without
recompense" (*Topics* 125a18).

"No free gifts" is a slogan of anthropologists and sociologists, but
at the same time it is a challenge to theology. The slogan can be interpreted to mean that every giver is promoting his or her self-interest
which is at stake in the reciprocal exchange. Even God giving freely to
the creatures is, in terms of this interpretation, attempting to win support or exercise power over creatures through creating relationships of
obligation and dependence. The language of gift giving has thus become vulnerable. Receiving a free gift means that the receiver becomes
dependent on the giver.

This language is powerful in various forms of marketing and advertising. Receiving a free sample or a small gift means that you come
under the influence of some product offered. Of course, many, perhaps
most, consumers are perfectly aware of this and can interpret the

meaning of free gifts in advertisements in the proper manner. It also belongs to the nature of free offerings to stress that "you are under no obligation to buy this product," although creating the need and the obligation is exactly what the advertisement intends to do.

For these reasons, employing the language of gift giving is ambivalent in theology. Critical and enlightened consumers are well aware of the obligations and dependencies hidden under the rhetoric of "free gifts." When we use the language of gift in theology, our hearers and readers may become skeptical. A free gift offered in religion may appear to many as a Trojan horse carrying some masked group interest under its surface.

But isn't the issue in reality more complex, and not only in religion, but already with regard to concrete gifts? A salesman is offering a free gift in order to create market opportunities. But if I give money to the Red Cross, or donate blood or become an organ donor, I have a completely different, unselfish intention to give. At the level of common sense, there apparently exist many forms of unselfish giving.

As we have seen, Marcel Mauss's approach was anti-utilitarian in the sense that the ancient habit of circulating gifts served many purposes, not only self-interest. Mauss attempted to show that human being is not necessarily a *homo oeconomicus*, a person who calculates everything in terms of utility. In the last chapter of *The Gift*, Mauss argues that in modern societies legislation, taxes, and social benefits take over some functions of the ancient gift. Thus there can emerge a balance between individual self-interest and collective well-being in a modern society. But the ancient habit of giving gifts already served both these purposes.

A contemporary Maussian could thus argue that two or perhaps three different institutions of circulating goods have taken over the functions of gift in a modern society. The first one is the market economy, that is, buying and selling with money. The market economy is the platform of *homo oeconomicus* in the strict sense. In addition to this, gifts served the purpose of mutuality and security in case of need. In modern societies, this second function is realized by the public sector. We have to pay taxes in order to finance healthcare, education, and other social benefits. These payments are necessary for the good of the society and its weaker members.

Neither of these two institutions is an example of free and unselfish giving. We may ask, however, whether in our societies there is a third sector or a third mode of circulation, motivated by generosity. In his book *The World of the Gift*,[2] Jacques Godbout argues that this third mode indeed exists and that in addition to the economic agent we can speak of *homo donator*, the human being who gives gifts and has genuine good intentions. For Godbout, the ancient idea of the gift is not exhausted by economic exchange and the public sector. In addition, there is gift giving which is not conditioned by legal or moral obligation nor by economic utility. Godbout claims that we observe this basic generosity in family life, in aid program, even in the habit of giving Christmas and birthday presents.

Godbout is certainly aware of the fact that most giving is in some way contaminated with consumerism and commercialism. But he attempts to show the other side of the coin. Sociologists after Mauss have shown that many kinds of obligations, dependencies, and exchanges are hidden under the manifest gift. Godbout claims, however, that under many forms of exchange we may discover a genuine act of giving, the paradigm of a gift. A Christmas present is not exhausted in being a part of commercial world and a form of exchange. There is an element or a surplus of sincere giving underlying whatever commercialism is involved. Likewise, the event of donating blood for the Red Cross is an obligation and in a sense similar to the event of paying taxes. By doing it one can guarantee that the society can meet some needs. But donating blood is more voluntary than paying taxes and there is an element or a surplus of generosity which cannot be understood in terms of exchange only.

So, the paradigm of gift is still present under the manifest exchange. In order to argue this, Godbout has to make some distinctions and qualifications. The generous gift underlying many forms of exchange is in some sense free. Many of us do not calculate in giving Christmas presents, and many of us, for instance children, receive presents freely and without feeling conscious obligations. On the other hand, this freedom cannot be explained in a full and strict sense. Giving a sufficient description of the freedom involved in a true gift probably in itself destroys the idea of the gift. A gift can be understood, but its freedom cannot be exhaustively explained.

---

[2] English edition: McGill-Queens University Press, 1999. The French original *L'esprit du don* appeared in 1992. The following summarizes some of the book's central argument. For a broader discussion of these ideas, see the French journal "La Revue du M.A.U.S.S." [Mouvement anti-utilitariste dans les sciences sociales], which seeks to develop the heritage of Marcel Mauss in a new fashion.

Another qualification concerns the reciprocity of the gift. For Godbout, even a true and spontaneous gift involves some reciprocity. A *homo donator* is nevertheless also a reciprocal agent. Reciprocity is already given in the phenomenon and in the concept: giving blood and giving a present gives you a feeling of happiness or delight, and in this way you already receive that feeling as a reward of your giving. Concerning the receivers (for example, children receiving Christmas presents), they also receive an understanding of what it is to give. In addition to the gift, children receive a model, and in learning this model they themselves learn to give. Receiving thus becomes a seed of further circulation. Godbout stresses that this circulation does not take place with any mechanical precision. We do not know how receiving prompts further giving. But the reciprocity nevertheless remains there in a manner which we cannot fully explain.

The story of my parents working in the farmer's field illustrates the strange phenomenon of reciprocity. My parents probably didn't calculate, but wanted to help out of generosity—or at least the trust they wanted to create was not calculated. They were troubled by the counter-gift not only because it obligated them, but also because they thought it was a waste of money. On the other hand, their voluntary help prompted spontaneous reciprocity, since after receiving the help a counter-gift emerged with the purpose of continuing the circulation. It is possible that the farmer didn't calculate either but donated the plate without scrutinizing his own motives. He did have some obvious motives, but the gift was nevertheless not strictly utilitarian. Perhaps the farmer, like the wasteful competitors in Mauss's study, even thought that the gift must be expensive in order to underline that it is not utilitarian, but a token of real hospitality.

Godbout rehabilitates a common-sense idea of the gift without completely separating it from the network of reciprocity observed by Mauss and other sociologists. He respects the intuition that people give freely and often do not calculate. At the same time, however, he admits our failure to explain this phenomenon in full detail. We obviously have good and unselfish intentions, but giving a sufficient reason for these intentions tends to contaminate the intention. In a sense, *homo donator* thus remains a mystery. Whereas the market economy provides a clear and simple calculative explanation of many forms of exchange, the phenomenon of the gift is an ideal type, a force whose effects we can observe and even understand but whose origin we cannot reach or explain.

For many sociologists, postulating a mysterious *homo donator* is too high a price to pay for an explanation of social phenomena. Pierre Bourdieu,[3] for instance, attempts to construct a notion of gift without referring to intentions and other subjective concepts. After Mauss, the structuralist approach to gift exchange focused on the equivalence between gift and counter-gift. Bourdieu adds the time factor to this discussion and can thus distinguish among the various forms of exchange. Giving the same thing back immediately is simply a refusal. Giving back immediately something else that nevertheless equals the thing given is an act of commerce, of buying and selling. Giving back the same thing later is a loan. But giving back a different thing later is a gift, Bourdieu claims. The counter-gift must be both deferred and different.

In many ways, Bourdieu's account makes much sense. Consider again the story of my parents. Giving back the fish plate to the farmer either immediately or next summer, instead of again volunteering for the harvest work, would have been a dramatic insult. Simply keeping the fish plate and disappearing next summer, instead of going to the fields, would also have been improper behavior. Mauss had already taken into account this time factor. If you had been invited to dinner at someone's home, you should wait a proper time before presenting an invitation to them. And you had better cook something different for dinner.

There is nevertheless something counter-intuitive in Bourdieu's description. The example of giving blood as an anonymous donor does not seem to fit into this scheme, since no counter-gift can be assumed. For Bourdieu, however, the whole theme of gift giving is embedded into a logic of practice which attempts to avoid the "ethnocentric" limitations of capitalist exchange. Unlike capitalist economies, archaic forms of exchange operate with symbolic goods or symbolic capital that is not limited to material value. On the contrary, sometimes extremely non-economic decisions are required in order to preserve the "symbolic alchemy," that is, the complex network of social obligations, traditions, and customs together with material and other needs. A person might, for example, buy a piece of land at an exorbitant price, given that it is connected to family history.

[3] Pierre Bourdieu, *Esquisse d'une théorie de la pratique* (Geneve:Droz, 1972); English: *The Logic of Practice* (Cambridge: Polity Press, 1980). For the sake of brevity, my following description is limited to the material available in *The Logic of the Gift*, ed., Alan D. Schrift (New York-London, 1997) 12–15 (Schrift's Introduction), 190–230 (selections from the Logic of Practice) and 231–43 (Bourdieu, "Marginalia—Some Additional Notes on the Gift").

A theory of practice thus has to pay attention to the matters of honor and social standing as well as other factors involving dependencies and power relationships. Bourdieu is opposed to purely speculative questions like "whether generosity is possible." One should concentrate on the economic and social conditions behind the habit of giving gifts. In the light of these conditions, even strange habits can be understood. Disproportionate gifts and seemingly generous offers receive a meaning within the social universe. A farmer giving a costly glass plate as a Christmas present to a distant urban family is an uncommon phenomenon as such. But once the social and economic needs of the farmer and the liaisons between giver and receiver are understood, the strange gift begins to make sense and to have a message.

Bourdieu stresses the hidden character of gifts and counter-gifts. The delayed reciprocity can only work if both sides act as if a unilateral pure gift were involved at each moment of the exchange. A "misrecognition" of the exchange is one of the principles underlying its effectiveness. A conscious aiming at an exchange would be harmful to the process. A farmer cannot say: "I give you this glass plate in order that I can count on your help next summer." A gift can consolidate the exchange only if it is misrecognized as a free gift.

Bourdieu and Godbout represent genuinely different sociological theories of the gift. What they have in common is, however, the task of explaining why people give gifts and the rejection of a straightforward "economic" explanation. Bourdieu is a pessimist with regard to true generosity, but he is an optimist in thinking that the practice of giving can be explained with the help of an understanding of the manifold and hidden social and economic conditions or "symbolic alchemy." Godbout is an optimist in thinking that genuine, altruistic gifts occur in many social relations, but he is a pessimist with regard to our possibility of explaining them in detail. Whereas the hiddenness of the gift is for Bourdieu a "misrecognition" belonging to the social practice at hand, it is for Godbout an unexplainable mystery, a force which we only know by its effects.

Sociological and anthropological findings have their obvious philosophical underpinnings. In order to reflect further on freedom and reciprocity, these concepts should be defined in detail. The social sciences are concerned with the real world with its dependencies and obligations, but philosophy focuses on the meaning of concepts.

From Derrida to Milbank: Given Time

In his book *Given Time*,[4] Jacques Derrida has presented the philosophical aporia of the gift in a concise manner. Derrida's argument can be summarized as follows: If I give you a gift, then I look good and put you in debt. But if this is to be a genuine gift, there "must be no reciprocity, return, exchange, countergift, or debt."[5] It makes no difference whether you give me something back now or later, for the very notion of the gift says that there is no giving back. In giving the gift, however, my social standing increases and you are placed in a debt of gratitude. Therefore, the "conditions of possibility of the gift . . . designate simultaneously the conditions of the impossibility of the gift." This is the fundamental aporia of the gift. It is basically not a social or economic circumstance, but a semantic or philosophical problem. It does not make sense to speak of gifts, since the act of giving takes from the recipient and adds to the donor, "which is the opposite of what the gift should do."[6]

Derrida thus sticks to the common-sense definition of the gift in a fashion similar to Godbout. But he immediately moves to prove that the common-sense definition entails a contradiction. Derrida remarks that Marcel Mauss is, paradoxically, not speaking of the gift, since he deals with economy, exchange, and contract. But the gift is, by definition, something else than these. Looking more closely at the situation, Derrida says that a mere recognition of the gift as gift by the receiver suffices to annul the gift. For in recognizing the intentional meaning of the gift, the receiver is already giving back something symbolic, namely, the recognition. Contrary to Bourdieu, Derrida does not think that this "something symbolic" would lead to a new circulation. The recognition of the gift by the donee adds to the donor, thus destroying the gift. In a similar fashion, neither should the donor know that she is giving a gift. As soon as the donor intends to give, she is starting to pay herself a symbolic recognition.[7]

---

[4] *Donner le temps, T.1, La fausse monnaie* (Paris: Galilée, 1991). English: *Given Time 1. Counterfeit Money* (Chicago: University of Chicago Press, 1995). The following description is based on *The Logic of the Gift* (= LG) 10–11 (Alan Schrift's Introduction) and 121–47 (Derrida, "The Time of the King," i.e., the first chapter of Given Time), as well as on the volume *God, the Gift and Postmodernism* (= GG), ed. John Caputo and Michael Scanlon (Bloomington: Indiana University Press, 1999). This book contains Derrida's and Jean-Luc Marion's commentaries and interpretations by other scholars.

[5] LG 128.

[6] GG 4.

[7] LG 130.

Therefore, in order that a gift can be given, both the giver and the receiver should forget it immediately. After dealing with the details of forgetting, Derrida concludes that the gift must not appear as a gift. Knowing the truth of the gift is sufficient to annul the gift. The philosophical analysis of Mauss's findings leads to an aporia, since Mauss claims that all gifts create bonds and obligations. But in order to become a gift in the first place, the gesture or token given must "untie itself from obligation, from debt, contract, exchange, and thus from the bind."[8]

Derrida's interest to the phenomenon of the gift is not, however, nihilistic. On the contrary, the philosopher is focusing on it because the gap between the common sense idea of the gift and the impossibility of its precise definition points towards something more general and philosophically important. For Derrida, "the gift is another name for the impossible, we still think it, we name it, we desire it," although we never encounter it. Although "a theory of the gift is powerless by its very essence," one should make the effort of thinking the "transcendental illusion of the gift."[9]

Without going much deeper into Derrida's philosophy, we may note that the issue of the gift is related to his general ideas of deconstruction and *différance*. Deconstruction is a method of critical scrutiny which finally leaves us with apories or impossibilities. *Différance*, meaning both difference and delay, denotes the complex phenomenon of realizing both that we grasp a meaning differently "before" and "after" reading the text and that in the text we do not find the presence of its topic, but only its "trace." In speaking of gifts, we name a trace of something, but on closer examination we do not encounter the gift, but only an illusion of it, already deconstructed and shown to be aporetic.

The sociological discussion was summarized by Mary Douglas (1990) with the slogan "no free gifts." The philosophical discussion of the 1990s can be understood as a critical semantic investigation of this slogan. Derrida's result is, on the one hand, that the slogan is a tautology, since already the concept of gift is an impossibility. On the other hand, however, Derrida has continued to emphasize the relevance of gift in a somewhat enigmatic manner. He claims not to have said that there is no gift. On the contrary, "its possibility is possible as impossible." Derrida claims that the gift cannot be known as such, "but it can

---

[8] LG 140.
[9] LG 141–2.

be thought of. We can think what we cannot know . . . There is something in excess to knowledge."[10] In this way Derrida's "illusion" at least argumentatively resembles Godbout's account of unexplainable force.

At this point we already begin to see why particularly the philosophical discussion on the gift has begun to interest theologians and philosophers of religion. After a century of anthropological and sociological reduction and philosophical deconstruction, the gift still occupies a prominent place in the discussion of the humanities and social sciences. Moreover, secular academics have begun to ascribe almost mystical predicates to the gift that shines behind the limits of explanation and knowledge.

Jean-Luc Marion, a philosopher with a distinct Roman Catholic profile, has in recent years elaborated a philosophy of "givenness," in which the discussion on gifts is continued in a far-reaching phenomenological fashion.[11] For Marion, it is the phenomenon of "givenness" that provides a philosophical clue for the understanding of the gift. Going back to the philosophical tradition of Martin Heidegger and especially to Edmund Husserl, Marion attempts to radicalize the distinction between intention and givenness. According to Husserl, we mean or intend objects, but these are only in part fulfilled or given to our actual experience and intuition.[12]

For Derrida, Husserl's distinction means that our speech can be liberated from the fulfilling givenness. Meanings and speech occur in the state of nonknowing, without a clue of what intuitions and what givenness is meant by the speech. Marion, however, takes the reality of givenness to be the philosophical starting-point from which Husserl's distinction can be radicalized. Instead of saying that our speech or intentions are only in part fulfilled by the phenomenon present or "given" to us, Marion claims that it is the extremely rich givenness of the phenomena which primarily encounters us. Speech and intention are imperfect tools which cannot fully grasp the overflow of givenness.

---

[10] GG 60.

[11] See Marion, *Dieu sans l'etre* (Paris: Fayard, 1982), English: *God Without Being* (Chicago: University of Chicago Press, 1991); *Réduction et donation* (Paris: PUF, 1989), English: *Reduction and Givenness* (Evanston: Northwestern University Press, 1998); *Etant donné* (Paris: PUF, 1997). The following presentation employs GG (see previous note) and Marion's article "Sketch of a Phenomenological Concept of Gift" (= SP), in: *Postmodern Philosophy and Christian Thought*, ed., Merold Westphal (Bloomington: Indiana University Press, 1999) 122–43.

[12] GG 6.

What we can get is a "saturated" intention, a treasure of meanings imposed on the ego by the overflowing givenness of the phenomena.[13]

This approach calls for a new way of thinking metaphysics and theology. Marion argues that an ontological theology, applying the "metaphysics of presence," is fundamentally misleading. An ontological approach remains captured in the Cartesian and Enlightenment modes of distinguishing between subject and object. But, Marion argues, we do not meet objects in their objectivity, but encounter the overflowing givenness. For instance, a phenomenon of birth is not fundamentally an object, but an extremely rich package of experiences and meanings, relating to continuity and change, to various persons involved, to one's new self-understanding as a parent or grandparent, and so on. A birth thus becomes a saturated phenomenon. Its truth is not in hospital statistics, but in the overflow of givenness which surrounds the participants.

When Marion claims that we should think God without "being," he is not referring to the death of God or to any other version of liberal theology. Instead, he claims that grasping God in terms of ontology is a false approach. Somewhat like Karl Barth or Hans Urs von Balthasar, Marion is opting for a consistent theology of revelation, in which revelation gives God without the alienating Cartesian category of objective being. Revelatory theology thus in a way equals givenness and radical phenomenology. In God, there is an excess of givenness which does not allow for any limited objectification. In this way, Marion is close to the so-called negative theology which claims that we cannot know what God "is."

Thus it is the givenness or "the name" that characterizes God to us, not God's being. Since the saturated phenomenon of givenness is central to Marion, he is one of the few contemporary theologians who has developed a consistent theology of giving and the gift. Marion's thinking will therefore occupy us also in the next chapters. Here we will only look at his interpretation of the gift in discussion with Derrida.

Givenness is the universal way in which all phenomena appear. Objects are constituted as a givenness of meanings and "in order to appear, a phenomenon must be able to give itself." Givenness is the "first level" in this phenomenal constitution of the world, whereas the gift is "the final trait of every phenomenon revealing itself."[14] We see that, for Marion, the gift has a fundamental philosophical significance.

---

[13] GG 6–8.
[14] SP 123.

Having the whole French discussion from Mauss to Derrida in mind, Marion asks whether we can have an appropriate concept of the gift. As a postmodern phenomenologist, Marion is philosophically close to Derrida. Approving Derrida's results at this point, however, would question the entire approach to givenness and the gift as philosophically fundamental concepts. Marion is sympathetic to Derrida's reading of the gift, but claims that he can do more. For Marion, the contemporary discussion is hampered by the "economic horizon" and the "metaphysical interpretation" of the gift. These destroy the phenomenological givenness which is the adequate perspective on the issue.

What Marion does is reconduct "the gift away from economy and towards givenness." The gift should be reduced to givenness by "bracketing" in turn the giver, the recipient, and the objectivity of the gift. What remains is the truth of the gift. In this process of bracketing, Marion finds first that in giving, it is the "givability," the self-decision and openness of the giver, which is fundamental. "The gifts which give the most give literally nothing," since in these it is the giver's self-decision what counts in the final analysis. In my giving this ring to you it is not the ring that finally counts, but my self-decision, of which the ring is a symbol. When a ruler gives up power, he is literally giving no object, but the ruler is nevertheless giving the most he can give.[15]

The same holds true in the bracketing of the recipient. When I make up my mind to receive something, the gift fulfills itself perfectly. It is not my coming to possess an object that is the final truth, but my openness, my decision to receive. These two self-decisions become then logically connected with the third reduction, namely, the reduction of gift to "that which itself gives." A gift determines itself as gift "through the double consent of the giver and of the recipient." For Marion, it is important that the gift is not regarded in terms of an object—that would lead to economic and metaphysical misreadings. Recognizing the gift as gift is not a mere objectification, but an instance of givenness or self-giving. The gift reduced phenomenologically to self-giving is not dependent on any extrinsic relation (for example, economic exchange), but it "takes its character of given from givenness alone."[16]

Marion is aware of the highly abstract level of this reduction and he attempts to formulate an ideal gift. Giving something to an enemy,

---

[15] SP 131–33.
[16] SP 137.

as Jesus teaches, fulfills the condition of bracketing the recipient, since an enemy does not feel indebted to the giver. Receiving something from an unknown giver fulfills the condition of bracketing the giver. The recipient feels indebted, but does not know to whom, and thus the debt is unsolvable. The gift reduced to givenness can thus be illustrated "as an unsolvable gift given to an enemy."[17] In this way Marion can reach an appropriate concept of gift. This concept is illustrated in my giving something anonymously to my enemy.

This result is both ingenious and strange. It obviously contains some theological underpinnings in the picture of giving a gift or even oneself to an enemy, as well as in the idea that we have received everything from an unknown giver. In addition, the step from giving to self-giving requires a closer analysis. For Marion, the gift "decides itself"; it can "determine itself as gift" and is thus a "self-giving" activity.[18] It is not a reification or personification of the gift that is intended here, but, on the contrary, the phenomenon in its overflowing richness. This phenomenological perspective is aware of the various meanings of the gift which, liberated from its metaphysical, objectivist, and economic straitjackets, can shine as a treasure-chest of intuitions. In this sense, it is the "final trait" of the phenomena revealing themselves.

Marion accomplishes a literal reading of Edmund Husserl's principle, according to which the phenomena are to be accepted just as they give themselves. The "givenness" implied in that principle makes all phenomena "self-giving" realities. Although it is not a personal "self" that is meant, one wonders in what sense the German word for givenness, *Gegebenheit,* and especially the German idiom *es gibt* (there is, but also: it gives), as developed by Martin Heidegger, lurk behind Marion's phenomenology of givenness.

This is one of the critical points that Jacques Derrida makes to Marion. In a recent discussion between the two, Derrida claims that Husserl and Heidegger did not relate their discussion on givenness to gifts. As technical terms of phenomenology, "givenness" and the "given" simply do not contain the broad connotations ascribed to them by Marion. In his reply Marion disagrees both historically and with regard to content. For him, the link between givenness and the gift is a development of Husserl's phenomenological method which

---

[17] SP 142.
[18] SP 136–37.

proves to be philosophically fruitful. "So givenness perhaps opens the secret, the final result and the potentially lost analysis of the gift."[19]

We need not here discuss the historical correctness of Marion's interpretation of Husserl, but his relationship to Derrida is instructive. Marion agrees with Derrida in the analysis that no explanation of the gift is possible in the horizon of economy. What Marion is doing, however, is a phenomenological description, and he claims that through the process of "bracketing" one can see new aspects that one cannot reach through remaining in the categories of object and being.

This is shown by the fact that you can describe a gift without a receiver, as in giving to an enemy or in giving anonymously to a humanitarian association. It is also possible to describe a gift without a giver, as in the case of inheritance. There is even the possibility of gift without any giver, as in the case of Robinson Crusoe who finds a tool on the sand. The tool might not be given at all, but is just luckily lying there. And a gift can be something wholly immaterial, like giving time or giving power.[20] For Marion, these descriptions are symptomatic of the primordial givenness of the world.

Marion is obviously employing "giving" and "givenness" as transcendental terms, that is, as conditions of possibility. Things simply cannot be, or be observed, if they are not able to give themselves to us. In this sense "the given facts" and perhaps even their self-giving precedes being and knowledge. Although this mode of speaking sounds like the German *es gibt*, it is also arguable in English, or at least it corresponds to some archaic linguistic uses and cultural practices, as John Milbank[21] has pointed out.

After Derrida, theologians have become more interested in the issue of gift and have increasingly contributed to the discussion. As we have seen, Jean-Luc Marion is a theologically interested philosopher. John Milbank, a philosophically interested theologian, has contributed to the topic of giving in various ways to which we will return later. At this point we will only briefly sketch his reply to Derrida and Marion, together with his own proposal for an adequate approach to gift exchange.

---

[19] GG 58–61

[20] GG 62–63.

[21] In his article "Can a Gift Be Given? Prolegomena to a Future Trinitarian Metaphysic," *Modern Theology* 1995, 119–22 (= CG). My following presentation of Milbank is based on this article and his book *Being Reconciled, Ontology and Pardon* (London: Routledge, 2003).

Milbank pays attention to the transcendental meaning of gifts and giving for both Derrida and Marion. Gift operates as a "regulative horizon" of statements concerning being. Things are to the extent that they give themselves. The extremely unilateral construal of true gifts in these approaches is an instance of "modern purism": the moment of exchange has to be deleted completely in order that a gift can be gift. But for Milbank, Marion's attempt to construct a pure gift without being, a pure givenness, becomes an absolutization of empty subjectivity. A gift without being cannot be a gift of anything.[22]

Although Marion claims to radicalize phenomenology, he remains finally bound to the Cartesian priority of the given. A "phenomenological passivity" of this kind does not allow us to see reality as givenness, but it amounts to an absolutized free subjectivity. Although the problems of subjectivism and nihilism haunt Derrida's account of the gift as well, Milbank is more sympathetic to Derrida, since his account is "the only possibly consistent fashion" of presenting a theory of unilateral gift. Marion's attempt is more problematic since it builds a theological variant—God and revelation as pure givenness—on the top of Derrida's aporetic result. But if God is presented primarily as gift or *summum bonum*, then God is reduced either to an ontic cause or an impersonal Neoplatonic One.[23] Thus Marion remains bound to the Cartesian categories of subject and object. The category of "givenness" is no shortcut to an adequate theology of revelation.

Milbank's criticism already reveals his own standpoint. He wants to rehabilitate ontology and, in addition, he claims that we finally, and also in theology, ought to see the gift in terms of gift exchange. Unilateral "purism" leads nowhere. Milbank emphasizes the findings of anthropologists and sociologists: a good and sensible gift does receive something back, as Mauss and others have shown. Although Milbank does not approve Bourdieu's understanding of a "theory of practice," he defends the view that gifts are characterized by a reciprocity involving time delay and non-identical repetition. This understanding is compatible with Christian love, agape. Agape is not unilateral "pure gift" but a "purified gift-exchange."[24]

We will come back to agape in the next chapter. Here we focus on Milbank's philosophical argument. He welcomes Marion's insistence

[22] CG 130–32, 137.
[23] CG 141–44.
[24] CG 125, 131. I will not italicize the most frequent non-English words, e.g., agape and mimesis.

on the distance between the giver and the receiver and the insight that in a sense nothing can be given to God in return for the divine gift. But Milbank claims that this supreme model of unilateral giving in reality involves some reciprocity. A gift makes the giver to be seen and so repeats the gift "backwards." Thus there is a "coincidence of absolute gratuity with absolute exchange." If the receiver is constituted by givenness and the gift, the receiver's insight and recognition of this state of affairs already is a sort of returning an acknowledgement. If this fails, the gift simply is not there and cannot be given. In order that a divine gift, the ideal model of the gift, can be given, both distance and reciprocity are needed. This gift exchange takes place with the help of delay and non-identical repetition which distinguish gift from contract.[25]

In this way Milbank argues that Marion's emphasis on "givenness" in fact does not support pure unilateralism but involves a moment of reciprocity. Only Derrida's nihilistic account of the impossibility of gift is consistently unilateral. Milbank in fact approves much of Marion's analysis, but with the massive change that being and reciprocity in some way precede givenness. Reasons for this change are to a great extent theological. The logic of creation demands "another ontology," not the ontology Marion is fighting against, but nevertheless an approach involving the notion of being. What is needed is "perhaps precisely an ontology of the gift."[26]

Our overview lets us see how complex the discussion of gift and giving from Mauss to Milbank in fact is. The first wave, stretching to Bourdieu and Mary Douglas, emphasizes the reciprocity. The second wave, here exemplified by Godbout, Derrida, and Marion, attempts at rescuing the "pure gift" with the help of a theoretical analysis. Milbank is the third wave, criticizing the second and attempting to define the gift with the aid of some results of the first wave, but claiming that reciprocity, time delay, and non-identical repetition finally operate on a higher level, at the level of agape. Archaic gift exchange (first wave) thus becomes transformed and purified into Christian agape (third wave). The nature of this agape can be philosophically supported through analyzing the shortcomings of the first and second wave.

It is further important to see some of the strategies of argumentation underlying this discussion. An anti-ontological approach is conjoined with a strict unilateralness of the gift (Derrida, Marion), whereas reciprocal approaches embrace a special ontology of the gift (Milbank) or

[25] CG 133–35, 144.
[26] CG 137.

social, economic, and anthropological theories (first wave). In a somewhat strange manner, theology is a latecomer in this discussion. Only after Derrida's analyses began to show theological aspects did different theologies (Marion, Milbank) start to develop around the issue of the gift. This is strange above all for the simple reason that "the gift" has been a prominent interpretative concept throughout the history of theology.

Concerning our initial example of the fish plate, contemporary philosophical views emphasize different aspects. Derrida might take the role of my troubled parents and say that they can analyze the fundamental aporias underlying our culture. Milbank would encourage all parties by insisting that this exchange can be elevated into a purified gift-exchange, in which both the farmer and the voluntary workers can get a sense of absolute gratuity through participating in the process. Marion might say that the most profound thinker in the story is my little brother. For he sees the beauty and richness of the fish plate and thus gets a glimpse of the saturated phenomenon.

What relevance does this rather philosophical and anthropological discussion have to ecumenical theology? We will investigate this issue in the next chapters and collect our results especially in the last chapter (ch. 6). But we may already point out that academics who are aware of the many faces of the gift tend to be skeptical when something is called a gift in a religious context. More importantly, this skepticism is not only a feature of academics but of many ordinary people of our postmodern age. In the midst of advertising, media, and commercialism, all offering different products and ideologies "for free," ordinary people have become critically aware of the rhetoric of free gift.

The so-called misrecognition, emphasized by Bourdieu and other theorists, is therefore not only an academic sophistication, but also a conscious attitude of ordinary people. We behave, and we know that we behave, as if our offerings and gifts were handed out in gratuity, although we know and the receivers know that they are not. "There is no free lunch." This attitude, which sometimes approaches cynicism, is so common that theologians and ecumenists simply have to be aware of it when they are proclaiming their message with the help of the rhetoric of gift.

One ecumenical text which may illustrate this state of affairs is the most recent Anglican–Roman Catholic common statement, *The Gift of Authority* (1999).[27] This text investigates the possibility that Anglicans,

---

[27] For the following, see *The Gift of Authority: Authority of the Church III* (New York: Church Publishing, 1999); *Communio sanctorum: Die Kirche als Gemeinschaft der Heiligen* (Frankfurt: Lembeck, 2000).

and perhaps other Christians as well, may approve the teaching authority of the pope. In their preface to this text, the co-chairmen of the commission emphasize the notion of the gift: "Rightly understood, authority in the Church is God's gift, to be received gratefully." The teaching authority of the pope is a "gift to be received by all the Churches and is entailed in the recognition of the primacy of the Bishop of Rome."

Interestingly enough, the document itself hardly uses the notion of the gift in its theological argumentation. Only under the very last subtitle, "Universal Primacy: A Gift to be Shared," is the notion of the gift reaffirmed: "The Commission's work has resulted in sufficient agreement on universal primacy as a gift to be shared for us to propose that such a primacy could be offered and received even before our churches are in full communion. . . . It will be an effective sign of all Christians as to how this gift of God builds up that unity for which Christ prayed" (§60).

These sentences entail no less than three mis-recognitions. The first one, very conscious and intentional, is to call the difficult issue at hand a gift. Given this misrecognition, the text can claim that submitting to the authority of the pope is not a loss, but a gain. This move is so obvious that any ordinary reader of the text can see it. Precisely for that reason the move becomes a problem. Ordinary readers think that the classical problems of obedience to the pope remain hidden under the new notion: simply calling this difficult issue a gift does not help.

The second mis-recognition concerns the emphasis of both anthropologists and the Second Vatican Council that in speaking of gifts we are not dealing with their unilateral reception but with a gift exchange involving many reciprocal acts. Anglicans are given papal authority and they offer their obedience in return. The document, however, does not mention this "giving in return," although it is tacitly implied in the concept of authority. More importantly, it is not this kind of gift exchange that was meant by the Council fathers in *Lumen gentium* (ch. 1). An ecumenical gift exchange should consist of both sides giving and receiving something from their own treasure of faith. In *The Gift of Authority*, however, the reciprocal notion of gift exchange is replaced by a unilateral gift. Anglicans should receive the gift as Catholics have already received it.

The third misrecognition concerns the vertical and the horizontal elements in this gift. In the text, the gift of papal primacy is displayed as a gift of God to all churches. Catholics have received it and the issue at hand is whether other churches can receive it as well. This issue is recognized. What is consciously misrecognized, however, is the fact that the dialogue is a horizontal process between two ecclesial communions, of which one has the gift and the other has not. The argument proceeding from the vertical perspective may be theologically sound, but in visible reality it means that the Catholic position becomes imposed on the Anglicans.

Although this may be what the Anglicans in fact want to have, an outsider cannot avoid the impression that the rhetoric of gift is only employed to conceal the actual horizontal process taking place. It is highly symptomatic that the simultaneous German Lutheran–Roman Catholic document *Communio sanctorum* does not even mention the concept of the gift in its discussion of papacy.[28] Since the notion of the gift is central and precious in Lutheran theology (ch. 2), Lutherans are careful not to overload or to misuse this concept.

These critical remarks are not meant in the first place to be antiecumenical or even my final word concerning *The Gift of Authority*. I have made the remarks in order to highlight the fact that many critical people will read such statements from the particular perspective created by the conceptual refinement of the gift as well as our awareness of commercial manipulation strategies.

Of course, the conceptual refinement described in this chapter not only causes problems but it also creates opportunities. Especially in Jacques Godbout's sociological analysis as well as in Jean-Luc Marion's and John Milbank's philosophical theology a rehabilitation of the gift is taking place. It is certainly not my intention to conclude this chapter by saying that we should abandon gift language in theology since it has become vulnerable. On the contrary, precisely because of this vulnerability to misunderstandings, the language of the gift may reveal to us theological dimensions which we could not otherwise detect. It is therefore the opportunities of the gift that will occupy us in the next chapters. First we will turn to some classical texts that have been influential in shaping our theological language of giving and the gift.

---

[28] *Communio sanctorum*, ch. VI, 4.

2

New Testament and Martin Luther

Didômi, the basic Greek verb "to give," occurs in the New Testament approximately 416 times, being one of its most frequent verbs. This state of affairs makes the treatment of biblical giving both fascinating and difficult. Fascinating, since *didômi* in addition to concrete giving and receiving often describes abstract, absolute, and divine giving especially in the Johannine writings. Difficult, because the verb appears in so many places that it is not easy to see the specific profile behind various usages. In its common and everyday meaning, the Greek *didômi* appears to be synonymous with both its Semitic counterparts and with many other and more recent Indo-European words for giving.[1]

The semantic relationship between giving and gifts (*dôron, dôsis*) is similar or perhaps slightly closer in biblical Greek than in contemporary English. A biblical gift is "what is given." Moreover, gifts and charisms are often characterized as given by God. Since the divine love, agape, is not only an attitude but an active and outpouring reality, God's love to humans is commonly portrayed in terms of gift and giving in the New Testament. This is already a basic reason why divine giving occupies a central place in so many biblical passages. God is love, and as love God is the giver. God is directly called the giver 104

[1] The following exegetical overview is based on many sources. I have used in particular: *Exegetical Dictionary of the New Testament*, eds., Horst Balz and Gerhard Schneider (Grand Rapids: Eerdmans, 1990); Klaus Wengst, *Das Johannesevangelium* 1–2 (Stuttgart: Kohlhammer, 2000–2001); Wiard Popkes, *Christus traditus* (Zürich: Zwingli Verlag, 1967); F. F. Bruce, *The Epistle of Paul to the Galatians* (Exeter: Paternoster Press, 1982); Richard N. Longenecker, *Galatians* (Dallas: Word Books, 1990).

times, of which 42 are in John's Gospel and John's Letters. In addition
to these, the so-called divine passive of the type "he was given the
power" (Rev 6:4) often occurs as an indirect reference to divine giving.
Jesus Christ is presented as the giver 68 times, of which 26 are in John.
Moreover, Jesus is portrayed as the receiver of what God gives 28
times in John.

Giving and Handing Over

The Gospel of John is thus our most prominent biblical source and
a fountainhead that has prompted theological reflection on giving and
gifts in Christianity. When we look closer at this terminology, an obvious starting-point is John 3:16: "For God so loved the world that he
gave his only Son." Jesus is here the gift given. The recipient is not
named, but the purpose of the act is clear: that the believers may have
eternal life. In later theology, the recipient is often understood to be
death. We will leave open the difficult issue in which sense the death in
such phrases is personified. However, "given [or given over] to death"
normally is expressed in the New Testament by another and related
verb, *paradidômi*. Sometimes, as in Galatians 1:4, *didômi*, too, may relate
to death, but the Johannine context (3:17) clearly indicates that it is not
just death, but the whole sending of Jesus to the world which is meant
by "gave" in John 3:16. The recipient is thus the world and the verse
underlines the similarity between sending and giving in John's
Gospel. God gave or sent his son to the world.

Sending and giving are also closely related in John 3:34-35: God
the Father, who has sent Jesus, has given the Son all things and gives
the Spirit without measure. Now the Son is the recipient, whereas "all
things" and the Spirit are the gift given. God's giving is still amplified
in John 3:27 where human beings become the recipients: "No one can
receive anything except what has been given from heaven." John 3
thus speaks of divine giving in a very comprehensive manner. God
gives "all things"; they are given to the Son; and human beings can
only receive them from above. The Son is both the recipient of all
things (3:34-35) and the gift which God gives to the world (3:16).
Human beings have received everything as a gift. This thought is already expressed by Paul (1 Cor 4:7).

John 4:10 identifies again the particular gift, the Son. In addition,
John 4 opens new dimensions of concrete and abstract giving. Jesus
has asked the Samaritan woman to give him a drink (4:7). After the

woman points to the fact that Jews do not share things with Samaritans, Jesus continues (4:10): "If you knew the gift of God, and who it is that is saying to you, 'Give me a drink,' you would have asked him, and he would have given you living water." In addition to the previous idea of Jesus as gift, we have him receiving water from the woman. He receives "all things" from the Father, and ordinary things, like a drink, from other humans. Thirdly, Jesus is now also a giver, namely the giver of "living water." John 4:14-15 enriches the idea of Jesus as giver. The water he gives to humans "will become in them a spring of water gushing up to eternal life."

In John 3–4 Jesus thus occupies all three places related to giving: first he is the gift of God to the world, then the recipient of all things, and finally the giver of living water. Throughout John's Gospel, Jesus keeps explaining the complex mutuality of giving, sending, and receiving. In 5:19-21, the analogy between the giving of the Father and the Son is described. "Whatever the Father does, the Son does likewise . . . just as the Father raises the dead and gives them life, so also the Son gives life to whomever he wishes." In such passages, giving is often generalized and abstract: the Son can give anything to anyone.

The analogy between Father and Son is not, however, symmetric but asymmetric in the sense that there must be the first giver. The Father is always the first giver, whereas the Son can only do "what he sees the Father doing" (5:19). The Son's giving is not spontaneous but it reflects the act of the Father. "I can do nothing on my own" (5:30). In sending the Son the Father has "given him authority" (5:27). The unity and equality of the Father and the Son is thus asymmetric in the sense that "giving" originates from the Father. As recipient, gift, and giver the Son sets the circulation of giving and receiving in motion. But giving is not a symmetrical cyclic motion without beginning. It has its definite origin and starting-point in God the Father. Through occupying all three places of the relationship of giving, the Son can become a mediator between the original giver and the world. From the perspective of the world all things are given in the sense that we can only receive them "from heaven." For John, the universe is structured by divine giving and sending, a process mediated to us by the Son.

John's Gospel often repeats this structure of giving with phrases that are abstract and complicated. In John 17:6, for instance, the identification of persons and messages is done in terms of manifold giving: "I have made your name known to those whom you gave me from the world. They were yours, and you gave them to me, . . . they know that everything you have given me is from you; for the words that you gave to me I have given to them, and they have received them . . ." In other words, Jesus is given a group of adherents from the world. They are a gift from the Father to the Son. But they are also recipients of another gift, namely of knowledge and the "words" which manifest the very structure of the process originating from the Father. This knowledge and these words, in particular "your name," become mediated through the process of giving and receiving.

One helpful way of understanding John's Gospel is to say that John depicts the human phenomenon of giving and receiving, or the whole process of gift exchange described in the previous chapter, and ascribes it to God and to our relationship with Jesus Christ. In giving and receiving gifts, there is both reciprocity and a final asymmetry at work. Our giving and receiving reflects and repeats previous similar acts. If this exchange is not just buying and selling, if there is a real gift underlying the process, then someone has initiated the circulation of gifts. If we are endowed with the gift of life which we have not bought and cannot trade, then there is somewhere a first giver of this gift.

Although this analogy from non-theological towards theological giving is helpful, it is nevertheless necessary to see the difference between divine and worldly giving in John's Gospel. When Jesus gives his peace (14:27), he adds: "I do not give to you as the world gives." Most commentators take this to mean that there are two different gifts, that is, two kinds of peace, worldly and divine. Literally, however, Jesus here speaks of two different modes of giving. This literal reading gets some support from the story of Samaritan woman (John 4), in which the concrete giving of a drink is contrasted with the giving of living water. What makes living water different is not the substance of the gift, but its coming from a different giver.

This structure of difference in giving is even more visible in John 6:31-39, where Jesus contrasts the bread of God with ordinary bread: "For the bread of God is that which comes down from heaven and gives life to the world" (6:33). The difference is not explained in terms of substance, but in terms of how the bread is given. Probably, however, in all these examples one must see the close relationship between giving and the gift. Reducing the difference either to the gift or to the act of giving is misleading. In John 6:33, the divine giving is emphasized, but when Jesus says in 6:35 that "I am the bread of life" he is the gift which makes the difference. Likewise, in the act of giving peace (14:27), the mode of giving goes together with the gift given. In the act of giving peace, this togetherness can be grasped already within the limits of ordinary giving: if I give you the sign of peace in a worship service, the gift is there in my very act of giving.

The eucharistic context of John 6:35 also illustrates the togetherness of gift and giving. The Eucharist is commonly understood as an act of self-giving, in which Jesus Christ is both the giver and the gift. We will return later to the complex topic of self-giving; here it suffices to say that in the act of self-giving one cannot strictly separate among giver, giving, and the gift. Of course it is in most cases nevertheless helpful to make a conceptual distinction among the various moments of the comprehensive act.

This brief outline of how *didômi* is employed theologically in John's Gospel serves as first milestone in our historical overview. In the history of Christian theology the parallelism between giving and sending and the asymmetrical equality between Father and Son have served as starting-points of later reflection on trinitarian theology. The Johannine insight that created beings receive everything from the Father through the Son has exercised strong influence on later theological understandings of creation and salvation. Here we cannot trace those influences historically, but we will see their effects in our later chapters when we treat forgiveness, salvation, and sacraments.

Another very important biblical issue concerns the already mentioned verb *paradidômi*, to "hand over," "deliver" or "pass on."[2] The Greek word denotes an intensified form of giving. The theological importance of this mode of giving is rooted in the fact that the verb is central in the passion accounts of the Gospels. In Mark 9:31 Jesus says that "the Son of Man is to be betrayed (*paradidotai*) into human hands," in 10:33 that he "will be handed over to the chief priests and the scribes . . . they will hand him over to the Gentiles." In 14:10, Judas "went to the chief priests in order to betray *(paradoi)* him to them." In Gethsemane Jesus says to the sleeping disciples (14:41): "The Son of Man is betrayed (*paradidous*) into the hands of sinners."

Mark's use of *paradidômi* has often been interpreted as follows: in its earliest usages this verb was probably non-theological, simply meaning the process by which Jesus was handed over to his enemies. But already in the above-quoted sayings of Jesus, the Gospel indicates a divine passive at work. These sayings are consciously enigmatic, pointing to the messianic secret which is slowly revealed. For these

[2] In the following I often share the opinion of Popkes 1967.

reasons, the giver in this process remains hidden. The reader can assume that God is, as hinted by the divine passive, delivering Jesus as a victim to the enemies. Jesus might also be himself the giver, thus performing an act of self-giving, that is, letting himself be handed over to the enemies. At the same time, however, there remains the concrete reading that it is Judas who hands Jesus over to the chief priests. *Paradidômi* has obvious legal meanings related to trials in general: a person can be handed over for judgment and punishment.

Among the great variety of Pauline usages of the verb, Romans 8:32 is thematically connected with passion stories: "He who did not withhold his own Son, but gave him up (*paredôken*) for all of us, will he not with him also give *(charisetai)* us everything else." As the context (32-39) shows, God's handing over Jesus brings justification (33) and the love of Christ (35) to all people. Here the focus is on the giver, namely God, but the recipients are left unstated. Is Christ also here handed over to the chief priests? If this word comes from tradition, and it probably does, then we may simply answer "yes." "All of us," however, are in some sense recipients. This sense is derived from the insight that Romans 8:32 as a whole speaks of God who gives us everything as a free gift. God's handing over his own Son is for Paul the utmost example of this comprehensive giving. Of course this idea does not reduce the salvific meaning of "for all of us": we certainly are beneficiaries of Christ's saving work. But the idea that we are recipients of the favor (verb *charizomai*) in which "everything else" is given implies that Christ is also given to us.

Thus the giving expressed in Romans 8:32 has slight similarities with John 3:16: in both the Son is given to us or to the world at the same time as he is given to death. The verb *charizomai* is connected with *charis*, grace or favor. For Paul, *charizomai* also has the meaning "to give." Here the verb underlines that "everything else" is given as a free gift or a gift of grace. The verb is not common in the New Testament, but in Philippians 1:29 it is used for saying that God has "granted you (*echaristhê*) the privilege not only of believing in Christ, but of suffering for him as well."

Theologically important in the use of *paradidômi* is, as we have seen, the fact that it interprets the death of Christ as a process of delivering or handing over Christ. There is an act of giving and receiving presupposed, but the placeholder for the giver and the placeholder for the receiver are to some extent left enigmatic. This structure of giving leads to classical dogmatic problems. If Judas in delivering Christ to the chief priests is only the visible giver, the real actor being God or Christ, then we are close to having a theory of a divine atonement or satisfaction. If God hands Christ over not only to the visible executors, but all of us are recipients of this act of para-giving, then all of us are in some sense involved in the death of Jesus.

We will not develop these dogmatic theories here, but have only pointed out in what ways the biblical vocabulary of giving opens the possibilities for developing these theories. It is important to notice that this is done by using the rhetoric of giving while leaving open the issue of defining the final giver and the ultimate recipient. As we saw in previous chapter, Jean-Luc Marion and other philosophers paid attention to the issue of "bracketing" the giver and the receiver. The New Testament use of *paradidômi* is an example of such bracketing, of the fact that we can speak extensively of giving without identifying the giver or the recipient.

As a last biblical point it should be noted that although we have above treated *didômi* and *paradidômi* separately, they sometimes come together and overlap. A condensed and dogmatically influential example of this is Galatians 1:4 and 2:20. In Galatians 1:4 Paul speaks of Jesus Christ "who gave himself (*dontos eauton*) for our sins to set us free from the present evil age." In 2:20 the same thought is embedded into the context of Christ present in faith. Now Paul uses the other verb: ". . . it is no longer I who live, but it is Christ who lives in me. And the life I now live in the flesh I live by faith in the Son of God, who loved me and gave himself (*paradontos eauton*) for me" Both verses are classical examples of Christ's self-giving, salvific action *pro nobis*, for our salvation. The "I" in Galatians 2:20 is an exemplary I, referring not only to Paul, but to Christians in general.

In these verses Christ is both the giver and the gift, whereas human beings are the beneficiaries; it is for their sake that the self-giving has taken place. The receiver is again bracketed. Since according to the commentators both verses come from pre-Pauline tradition, Jesus's giving himself to the chief priests and to death is at least indicated. Jesus's giving himself to all humans is in these verses somewhat ambivalent, since one cannot see any parallel idea to the Johannine "sending." Jesus gives himself to death, not to the world in general, although humankind benefits from this self-giving. But the beneficiary, as the final purpose of this giving, must be conceptually distinguished from the one to whom something is given.

On the other hand, the emphasis on God's agape in 2:20 is similar to the idea expressed in Romans 8:32, namely, that Jesus's self-giving is an extreme instance of God's gift-love extending to all humankind. The Christ who has given himself to death is now the Christ who lives in me by faith and through his love. I have thus received Christ by faith. In this sense Christians are receivers of this act of love's self-giving, although the literal "handing over" is done to the chief priests and to death.

What is important for us, however, is to see that giving, self-giving, and handing over are all employed in order to highlight the work of Christ for our salvation. The New Testament verbs *didômi* and *paradidômi* thus have a central soteriological use. They do not yet contain any elaborated theory of redemption or atonement, although they certainly prompt a historical development towards dogmatic definitions. If John's use of *didômi* prompted a later elaboration of the relationship between Father and Son, that is, of trinitarian theology, then the synoptic and Pauline use of *paradidômi* can be said to have promoted the later development of our understanding of Christ's work. Biblical origins of both trinitarian theology and soteriology are therefore closely connected with the peculiar use of the verbs expressing giving, self-giving, and handing over.

In biblical times, the topic of giving and receiving was also prominent in Stoic philosophy. A contemporary of Jesus and the apostle Paul, the Roman philosopher Lucius Annaeus Seneca devoted his study *De beneficiis* to the issue of giving and receiving favors, benefactions, and gifts, all of which are indicated by the Latin word *beneficium*. We will not treat Seneca in detail, but it is important to notice two things. First, many Christian writers, for instance Thomas Aquinas in his treatment of gifts in *Summa theologiae* II/2 q106, follow Seneca's views. Second, these views show resemblances to the contemporary discussion outlined in chapter 1. Thomas discusses the question whether one should return a favor immediately (q106 a4). He replies, quoting *De beneficiis* 4,40, that a person who immediately returns the gift has the mind of a debtor rather than of a true giver. Like Pierre Bourdieu and others, Thomas and Seneca advise people to wait a proper time before giving a counter-gift. Even Marcel Mauss's problem of the escalation of counter-gifts is present in Seneca (*De benef.* 1,4,3) and Thomas (*Summa theol.* II/2 q106 a6) who teach that one must give back more than what one has received. Otherwise the counter-gift would look like a payment. As with Mauss, gifts and favors are for Seneca "a matter which . . . holds human society together" (*De benef.* 1,4,2).

Unlike Mauss, however, Seneca defends the view that favors and gifts are free. Giving a favor is "purely a matter of paying out. Any return is sheer gain; if there is none, no loss is incurred. I gave for the sake of giving. Favors are not something which one enters into an account book . . . A good man never thinks of them, unless reminded by their return" (*De benef.* 1,2,3). Similar to modern philosophers, the giver's forgetting is necessary for the pure gift. Without entering Seneca's discussion in more detail, it can be said that the Hellenistic discussion of gifts and favors was sophisticated and paid attention to many of the issues we have treated in chapter 1. Even though biblical discussions of gifts and giving are not as such philosophical, we can assume that these phenomena were not treated in a naive fashion. It is more likely that people of different ages and cultures have been well aware of the social liaisons and networks defined in terms of gifts, favors, giving, and receiving.

It is not the topic of this book to examine the various forms of this doctrinal development. We may just mention that in the Nicene Creed, God the Father is called *poiêtes*, "maker" of heaven and of earth. The word also means a poet, and it stresses God's gift given in creation. In classical Greek philosophy, *poiêsis* is an act of producing a concrete object which continues its existence even in the absence of the producer or poet. In that sense, *poiêsis* resembles the act of giving gifts.

Recent attempts to outline a "poietological theology" emphasize that God is not only an authority and a cause behind the world. God is rather the author, a *Deus poeta* who is present in creative and constitutive word and communicates with us through the world. God's being is in this sense a "communicative gift."[3] Accordingly, the world is in some sense a product or a gift that continues to be on its own, although it is fundamentally dependent on the creator or the giver. Through the credal notion of *poiêtes*, God's giving and self-giving become connected with artistic creativity.

Another credal formulation which develops John's view of a Son to whom the Father has given everything is the phrase "begotten from the Father." Both the original Greek *ek tou patros gennêthenta* and the Latin *ex patre natum* contain the idea of "being born from the Father." This genetic relationship is able to highlight both the full equality and the fundamental asymmetry of Father and Son in John's Gospel. Father and Son are of same kind because one can beget the other, but it is nevertheless only the Son that is begotten or born. The biblical relationship of giving from the Father to the Son is thus prominent in the

[3] See Oswald Bayer, *Gott als Autor. Zu einer poietologischen Theologie* (Tübingen: Mohr, 2000) esp. 1–18, 118–22.

Nicene Creed within the semantically rich idea of a father "giving birth" to a son.

The notion *paradidômi* does not appear in the Nicene Creed, but the phenomenon of handing over comes into view when Jesus Christ is described: "he came down from the heavens and became incarnate from the holy Spirit and the virgin Mary, became human and was crucified on our behalf under Pontius Pilate; he suffered and was buried and rose up on the third day in accordance with the scriptures." This narrative of passion and resurrection advances through various stages. Jesus is first handed over from the heavens to the world, then he is handed over under the rule of Pontius Pilate, and finally passed on to the grave. Although there is not much explicit theory of salvation in this part of the creed, it is clear that the delivery of Jesus through these stages follows a specific pattern within the salvation history. "Handing over" Jesus thus contains a message which speaks of the plan of salvation manifesting God's gift of love.

When the biblical creeds and the basic biblical texts are explained in the history of Christian theology, the fundamental importance of giving is often emphasized. Moreover, the implicit presence of giving in the creeds again becomes explicit. We will investigate this process through concentrating on Martin Luther's catechisms as well as on his exposition of Galatians 1:4 and 2:20. There are several reasons why Luther is highlighted. He is an influential historical figure whose writings, in particular the catechisms, have shaped the whole of Protestantism. Luther is an ecumenically important theologian, whose catechesis and biblical exposition continues the medieval Western tradition, but also shapes the emerging early modern European thought.

Luther on Giving

My basic reason for describing Luther's position is, however, that he programmatically develops a theology of giving. This has been noted by specialists,[4] but contemporary theological discussion on gifts and giving has nevertheless utterly neglected Luther's contribution. One reason for this neglect may have been that authors like Jean-Luc

---

[4] Martin Seils, "Die Sache Luthers," in: *Lutherjahrbuch 1985*, 64–80; Simo Peura, "What God Gives Man Receives: Luther on Salvation," in *Union With Christ* (= UWC), ed. Carl Braaten and Robert Jenson (Grand Rapids: Eerdmans, 1998) 76–95; Sammeli Juntunen, "The Notion of 'Gift' (donum) in Luther's Theology," in *Luther between Past and Present*, eds., Ulrik Nissen et al. (Helsinki: Luther-Agricola-Society, 2004) 53–69.

Marion and John Milbank (ch. 1) are not close to Lutheranism. But probably Luther has also been regarded as an uninteresting thinker in this respect. Therefore it is my aim to show that he is both interesting and important. An ecumenical theology of giving and gift exchange may profit from Luther's contribution.

Luther is well aware that the trinitarian creeds have refined the New Testament language of giving. In his catechetical writings he aims at returning to biblical language and terminology. Of course he fully accepts the trinitarian doctrine, but he thinks that this very doctrine can be expressed to common people in biblical language. In his *Confession*, written in 1528, he summarizes trinitarian faith as follows:

> These are the three persons and one God, who has given himself to us all wholly and completely, with all that he is and has. The Father gives himself to us, with heaven and earth and all the creatures, in order that they may serve us and benefit us. But this gift has become obscured and useless through Adam's fall. Therefore the Son himself subsequently gave himself and bestowed all his works, sufferings, wisdom, and righteousness, and reconciled us to the Father, in order that restored to life and righteousness, we might also know and have the Father and his gifts.
>
> But because this grace would benefit no one if it remained so profoundly hidden and could not come to us, the Holy Spirit comes and gives himself to us also, wholly and completely. He teaches us to understand this deed of Christ which has been manifested to us, helps us receive and preserve it, use it to our advantage and impart it to others, increase and extend it. He does this both inwardly and outwardly—inwardly by means of faith and other spiritual gifts, outwardly through the gospel, baptism and the sacrament of the altar, . . .[5]

In this text, the trinitarian creed is rewritten from the perspective of God's self-giving. Already in the poietic, or creative work the Father performs an act of self-giving. Although the creation is a product distinct from its maker, it is sustained by the presence of God. The gift-character of creation is seen in the fact that creatures "serve and benefit" us. It is not the perspective of man's domination over creation, but the perspective of us receiving this gift. The articles of redemption and sanctification renew this perspective by taking into account sin, evil, and hiddenness. The self-giving of the Son and the Spirit enable

[5] Luther's *Works, American Edition*, vol. 37, 366 (LW). Martin Luther's *Werke, Weimarer Ausgabe*, vol. 26, 505–6 (WA). In the following I will quote Luther according to the LW, if available. For confessional texts, I will use the *Book of Concord* (= BC), eds., Robert Kolb and Timothy Wengert (Minneapolis: Fortress, 2000).

human beings to become receivers and preservers of God's gifts in our imperfect and sinful world.

One interesting feature of this text is that the article on the Holy Spirit provides an added value to the process of giving and receiving. We are to impart the gift to others, increase, and extend it. The receivers are called to circulate the gift. They may use it to their "own advantage" but at the same time the gift needs to be circulated and increased. Since the gift in question is "this deed of Christ," one may read the passage as referring to the proclamation and spreading of knowledge of Christ. But the deed of Christ described here is not only a message, but the whole process of "knowing and having" the gifts given already in creation. The circulation initiated by the Father's and the Son's self-giving thus comprehends the gifts themselves.

Trinitarian theology was not one of the debated issues in the Reformation. For that reason it provided Luther with a starting-point from which he could outline Christian theology without polemics. Luther's most influential treatises on trinitarian theology are contained in the expositions of the Apostles' Creed in *the Large* and *the Small Catechism* (both 1529). These text belong to the *Book of Concord*, the normative collection of Lutheran Confessions and they have been used as the most important pedagogical texts in Lutheranism until today. For these reasons alone, they deserve to be studied more closely.

The exposition of the Creed in *the Large Catechism* follows many ideas outlined in the *Confession* of 1528. The central notion is again that of giving. Believing in God the Father means that God "has given me and constantly sustains my body, soul, and life." God "gives all temporal and physical blessings—good government, peace, security." For Luther, everything is "daily given, sustained and protected by God." Our duty is to respond to all this giving through loving, thanking, and praising God for all these gifts. People may not respond this way in fact, but if human beings "practice this article" their hearts will be warmed and they may get "a desire to use all these blessings."[6]

We see here that the structure of giving and receiving is central to believing in God the Father. Luther and Lutheranism struggle with the sense in which human beings can respond to this gift, but at least in *the Large Catechism* Luther believes that practicing this process of reception may lead to a sort of therapy of the heart and its desires.

[6] BC 432–33.

In the second article concerning the Son, we know how God "has given himself completely to us, withholding nothing." Redemption is thus seen as an emptying of God. If the first article expresses rich divine giving which nevertheless does not exhaust all its possibilities, the second article for Luther means that in Jesus's self-giving nothing was withheld. The third article describes the Holy Spirit who makes us holy through offering to us and bestowing on our hearts the knowledge of Christ. Being made holy thus means "bringing us to the Lord Christ to receive this blessing, to which we could not have come by ourselves."[7] Here again Luther's struggle with the human non-capacity of reception is visible. It is important to notice that the office of the Holy Spirit concentrates on the opening of this human capacity for reception.

Luther's catechisms begin with the Ten Commandments and follow with this exposition of the Creed. This structure corresponds to the distinction between law and gospel, which is explained in terms of giving: ". . . the Creed is a very different teaching than the Ten Commandments. For the latter teach us what we ought to do, but the Creed tells us what God does for us and gives to us . . . . We see here in the Creed how God gives himself completely to us, with all his gifts and power, to help us keep the Ten Commandments: the Father gives us all in creation, Christ all his works, the Holy Spirit all his gifts."[8]

Being aware of all qualifications and restrictions that Lutheranism traditionally has had concerning therapeutic language, we may compare this theology of giving to a dialogue between doctor and patient. The doctor gives the medicine; the patient does not heal himself but he nevertheless should be open to receive help from outside. A therapist must first convince the patient that he is ill and then inform him of the treatment that is available. In the *Catechism*, the first step is taken with the Ten Commandments, which are employed for diagnostic purposes. The second step, informing and bringing the patient to the doctor, is the task of the Holy Spirit. Only then can the Father and the Son provide the actual treatment. Of course, "then" does not here refer to a temporal sequence, but to the logical sequence applied in the *Catechism*.

Each of these instances is described in terms of giving. In addition to the three persons, the Ten Commandments serve as a fourth instance. The Decalogue is the first instance of therapeutical sequence, but also in

---

[7] BC 434–36.
[8] BC 440.

a sense the last one, since the whole treatment is done in order to "help us keep" the commandments. Obviously, the commandments are also given by God. But what is characteristic in *the Large Catechism* is the presentation of the Creed in terms of such comprehensive divine giving.

The Small Catechism presents the same idea in an extremely condensed fashion. Oswald Bayer has shown how Luther's brief exposition of the first article moves among various circles of giving.[9] The first sentence of the Apostles' Creed is summarized as follows: "I believe that God has created me together with all that exists." This summary consists of three circles of divine giving: (1) body and soul: "God has given me and still preserves my body and soul; eyes, ears, and all limbs and senses; reason and all mental faculties; (2) daily bread and human needs: "God daily provides shoes and clothing, food and drink, house and farm, spouse and children, fields, livestock, and all property"; (3) protection: "God protects me against all danger and shields and preserves me from all evil."[10]

After this description of God's giving, Luther continues with the description of the giver and the receiver: "All this is done out of pure, fatherly and divine goodness and mercy, without any merit or worthiness of mine at all! For all of this I owe it to God to thank and praise, serve and obey him."[11] We can here note basically the same structure of giving and receiving as in *the Large Catechism*. God is the giver. We are recipients of God's goodness. And this reception is on the one hand not our "merit or worthiness," but on the other hand it takes place and should lead to thanksgiving and service.

Perhaps more strongly than in *the Large Catechism*, Luther here stresses that the divine giving is a continuous act without which human beings would be swallowed by non-being, that is, by the lack of all goods necessary for life and peace. Oswald Bayer remarks in his analysis that already in confessing this "categorical giving" of God, the believer participates in the responsive act of praise and thanksgiving.[12] But it is nevertheless also important that the sentence of explicit praise, thanks, and service be added in order that the response of humanity is not ignored. Praise and service witness to the productivity and fruitfulness of the faith of Christians. The believer thus participates in circulating the gift given.

[9] For the following, cf. Oswald Bayer, *Schöpfung als Anrede* (Tübingen: Mohr, 1990) 89–108.

[10] BC 354.

[11] BC 354–55.

[12] Bayer 1990, 107–8.

Luther's understanding of God the giver is both biblical and cate-chetical. Fundamentally, this understanding reveals the nature of Luther's whole theology of God's self-giving act. We can see this from his exposition of Galatians 1:4 and 2:20 in the *Greater Commentary on Galatians*. This commentary is an interesting source both because of its depth and because it is regarded by the Lutheran confessions as an au-thoritative description of the doctrine of salvation.[13]

Luther is not particularly interested in the traditional problem of asking to whom Christ was handed over (1:4) or to whom he gave himself (2:20). He repeatedly says that Christ was given to death for the sake of our sins. He says in his exposition of 2:20 at least once that Christ was sacrificed to God, thus leaning to Anselm of Canterbury's view of satisfaction as restoring God's honor. In the context of 1:4, however, Luther stresses that our "slavery under sin" (Rom 7:14) wit-nesses to Satan's power. He also refers here to the spiritual battle against evil powers, calling upon the classical idea of redemption as a battle between God and Satan in which the "handing over to death" was the strategy leading to the final victory over Satan and death.

Luther is not critical of these classical theories, but he is massively questioning the medieval idea of Christ as judge and legislator. Satan's strategy is to make Christ look like a cruel judge and thus to turn people to desperation and away from God. But Christ is not a deman-der, but a giver. He is not a judge, but a healer and a mediator. "He is not a tormentor. He is not one who will cast down the troubled, but one who will raise up the fallen and bring propitiation and consolation to the terrified." The human reason would bring to God "one who is well, not one who has need of a physician."[14] We meet again the therapeutic perspective from which the perspective of a legislator is criticized.

Here we have at work the classical Lutheran distinction between law and gospel. God seen under the law expects our good works. But we should not meet God as legislator, but as mediator and healer. Jesus Christ brings this perspective in his self-giving act of salvation. The true understanding of Galatians 2:20 must be seen in terms of God as giver: "Therefore Christ is not Moses, not a taskmaster or a lawgiver. He is the dispenser of grace, the savior, and the pitier. In other words, he is nothing but sheer, infinite mercy, which gives and is given. Then you depict Christ correctly."[15]

---

[13] LW 26, 32–42, 167–79. BC 573.

[14] LW 26, 39, 34.

[15] Ibid., 178.

There is yet another dimension of this self-giving. Christ is giving himself to death, and in that sense Christ is giving himself as the sacrifice needed for redemption. But when Paul says in Galatians 2:20 that Christ "loved me and gave himself for me," this means that the exemplary "me," all Christians, are also in a sense receivers of Christ. Of course Christians are the beneficiaries of the sacrifice done "for me" or "for all of us." But in Luther's view, Christians also receive Christ in this act of love. The medium of this receptive act of the Christian is faith: ". . . faith grasps and embraces (*apprehendit et involvit*) Christ, the Son of God, who was given for us, as Paul teaches here. When he has been grasped by faith (*apprehenso per fidem*), we have righteousness and life."[16] It is the act of apprehension through which Christ is received.

Luther thus connects Christ's self-giving with the first part of Galatians 2:20, in which Paul says that "it is no longer I who live, but it is Christ who lives in me." In the exposition of this verse Luther says that by faith "you are so cemented (*conglutineris*) to Christ that he and you are as one person, which cannot be separated but remains attached to him forever and declares: I am as Christ. And Christ, in turn, says: I am as that sinner who is attached to me, and I to him."[17] Through receiving Christ by faith, we have union with Christ. The gift is given for us, but also to us.

In sum, we see that Luther's exposition of the self-giving expressed in Galatians 1:4 and 2:20 stresses the reception of the gift given. Christ gave himself to death, but we are also the receivers of this act of redemptory self-giving. This is so because this act of Christ is basically an act of love by which Christ loves us. In this way we have a "Johannine" perspective of love in the middle of Luther's exposition of Paul. The act of self-giving is not only an abstract act of economic or forensic redemption, but it is basically an act of gift-love, in which we are not only beneficiaries, but also recipients of this love.

In fact, the conceptual difference between recipient and beneficiary is an important one. The three moments of a basic act of giving include (1) the giver, (2) the gift, and (3) the recipient. But some specific varieties of giving, in this case the sacrifice, presuppose a fourth moment, (4) a beneficiary for whose sake the act is performed. In my act of donating blood the Red Cross is the recipient (3), whereas some sick person is the beneficiary (4). Likewise Christ was handed over to death

---

[16] Ibid., 177.
[17] Ibid., 168.

for our sake, and thus death is the recipient (3) and we are the beneficiaries (4) of this sacrifice. Luther is saying with Paul that this act of
self-giving is not only *pro nobis*, an act done for our sake (4), but also an
act with results *in nobis* (3) when Christ lives in us. The intimacy between sacrificial giving and loving leads to the theological result that
beneficiaries (4) are also receivers (3). We will return to this issue in
chapter 4, but it is already here important to see the difference between
the recipient and the beneficiary. Given this conceptual difference the
same being can, however, in some cases be both the recipient and the
beneficiary.

We conclude our discussion of Luther with a path that highlights
the intimate relationship between God's giving and God's love. A pure
love would require a person who is not seeking his own profit but
would act altruistically. Giving a completely free gift would be an example of pure love and altruism. We saw in chapter 1 how difficult it is
for contemporary thinkers to construe a pure gift. Luther shares this
skepticism with regard to pure love and genuine altruism. For Luther,
human reason is inevitably egoistic and thus incapable of pure giving.
This incapability is not in the first place an issue of moral criticism, but
it is a description of the basic condition of human reason and our being
as humans. Therefore Luther's discussion of pure love and egoism
contains interesting parallels to the contemporary discussion.

Luther is always and tirelessly making the point that all human ef-
forts to do good and to live a good life are contaminated by egoism. If
natural reason claims that it can give free gifts or create objective justice, this is simply not true. A closer analysis of human action always
reveals the underlying egoism. Analytical reason can thus explain why
things go wrong, but it cannot become the source of true goodness. In
modern, or postmodern, terms, reason's task is deconstructive rather
than constructive. We can briefly look at Luther's deconstructive
analyses of two conceptual instruments of practical reason: first, the
notion of prudence, and second, the golden rule of reciprocity.

For Aristotle and for medieval philosophy and theology, prudence
was the virtue employed in good human action. A prudent person
finds the concrete ways and means to put his or her good principles in
practice. In Aristotelian thought, the natural reason of an educated
person is able to act prudently. Luther radicalizes and deconstructs
this view. He interprets Romans 8:7 to mean "carnal prudence," since
the apostle Paul is not dealing there with theoretical wisdom but with
practical reason as related to action. For Luther, carnal prudence is al-

ways directed towards choosing one's own good and avoiding the common good. Only spiritual prudence (Rom 8:6) can choose between good and evil.[18]

In his exposition of Romans 8:7, Luther describes how God gives everything as a gift: health, power, our intellectual skills, and our spiritual gifts. "Carnal prudence" twists all these so that the human being seeks his own good rather than the common good.[19] Of course, these are still good gifts, but since the common prudence of the philosophers is entangled in each of us with our carnal and egoistic prudence, things go wrong.

This does not mean that carnal, or natural, prudence is now simply a vice. Human reason is an especially good gift of God. Even a spoiled use of this gift does not extinguish the gift as such. Luther can for instance claim that it is better for a society to have a morally bad ruler who is prudent than to have a morally good but imprudent ruler. In the latter case, ruling simply does not work and results in anarchy. In the former case, the ruler is able to control concrete situations and thus can prevent anarchy. He is not, however, ruling for the sake of common good, but finally seeks his own profit. But even in this egoistic control, the power of gifted reason to bring forth an order which is better than anarchy is manifest.[20]

In this way the Aristotelian virtue of rational prudence is deconstructed and revealed to be "carnal prudence," a corrupted gift of God. Carnal prudence may claim to seek the common good, but in reality it seeks one's own profit and remains an ambivalent attitude, a perverted gift. Only spiritual prudence can overcome this ambivalence. But spiritual prudence is not a way of reasoning. It results from receiving God's gift properly, whereas carnal prudence twists and spoils this gift.

A similar, deconstructive procedure is visible in Luther's treatment of the Golden Rule: "In everything do to others as you would have them do to you; for this is the law and the prophets" (Matt 7:12). Since Augustine, this rule of neighborly love was interpreted in terms of the so-called *ordo caritatis*, the order of love. According to this order, you should love better things more. Among the various beings in the universe, God is the best and thus you should love God above everything else. In loving other humans and yourself, you should love soul more than body, since soul is better than body. The basic criterion of

[18] LW 25, 350–51.
[19] LW 25, 351.
[20] WA 20, 553.

the order of love is the inherent goodness of the object of your love. The Augustinian view is theological, but natural reason can understand it, since it reflects the natural ordering of values and degrees of goodness.

Luther is critical of this order of love, because its starting-point allegedly is the human being who evaluates the objects of the universe and then loves them according to this evaluation. This evaluation, however, reflects the character of human will and human values, which are inevitably selfish. What the human being considers to be the true order of goodness in the universe is thus conditioned by selfish desire. This is, as Antti Raunio has shown in detail, Luther's criticism of the Augustinian order of love.[21]

If one applies the Golden Rule according to the Augustinian order of love, then human self-love becomes the rational criterion from which one can proceed to understanding the eternal and at the same time natural love present in the universe. For Luther, however, natural self-love is a fundamentally misleading starting-point. Since human self-love always seeks one's own good, it cannot teach us anything of the true love which permeates the universe. When Luther interprets the Golden Rule, he therefore does not proceed from one's own expectation or desire, but from another starting-point, the perspective of what humans need and lack.

We may note in passing that Luther's critical deconstruction contains a parallel to Jean-Luc Marion's method of "bracketing" the participants of giving. Both Luther and Marion see the world as "given" and consider the perspective of the human subject to be misleading. It should be bracketed and replaced by comprehensive givenness, within which giving is separated from one's own desires and made anonymous. Luther, however, in my view radically differs from Marion in the issue of God's being or presence. Luther's exposition of Galatians 1:4 and 2:20, for instance, show clearly that he is not abolishing a "metaphysics of presence," but, on the contrary, developing a theological, or christocentric, ontology. Concerning ontology, Luther is thus closer to Milbank than to Marion.

For Luther, the Golden Rule actually tells us to give to others what they need. It is not a law of desire, yearning, and aspiration, but a rule

---

[21] I follow here Antti Raunio, *Summe des christlichen Lebens: die Goldene Regel als Gesetz der Liebe in der Theologie Martin Luthers* (Mainz: Philipp von Zabern, 2001). See also his "Natural Law and Faith: The Forgotten Foundations of Ethics in Luther's Theology," in *UWC*, 96–124.

telling us how we understand what our neighbor needs. It is a law of gift-love, a law of giving to others what they need. One way of emphasizing the difference between Luther and Augustine is to say that in Matthew 7:12 the starting point of Augustine is the Greek word *thelête*, expressing the will or desire: "what you would have." For Luther, the starting-point is *poieite*, "do [creatively, filling the need] to others," the verb expressing the creative or productive doing.

In their formulation of the Golden Rule, both Matthew and Luke (6:31) employ the verb *poieô* which at least since Aristotle expressed the emergence of a gift or product, that is, something that was not there previously. From this perspective one can read the Golden Rule so that the need of the "others" is fulfilled by the poietic gift. The verb *poieô* can also express a more general sense of doing; therefore the occurrence of this verb alone does not justify Luther's interpretation of it. But one can say that Luther's interpretation opens a viable alternative to Augustine's reading.

Antti Raunio remarks that Luther's need-based interpretation was already present to some extent in Gregory the Great and in Francis of Assisi.[22] It was in that sense not Luther's invention, but a minority opinion in the Western theology dominated by Augustine's desire-based theory of the order of love. Fundamentally, the Golden Rule is for Luther a "law of divine love." God does not simply love better things more. Instead, God's agape aims at fulfilling the creation's needs and wants. God outpours creative agape on the universe where it is lacking perfection.

Divine love is thus not an evaluation of the inherent value of its object. Instead, as Luther says in the concluding theses of his *Heidelberg Disputation* of 1518: "The love of God does not find, but creates that which is pleasing to it. The love of man comes into being through that which is pleasing to it."[23] God is thus able to love even emptiness and the sinner—and this is the capacity of agape to fulfill the imperfections and needs of the universe.

When Christians try to live according to the Golden Rule, they should imitate this love, the rule of divine love. Humans should meet their neighbor's needs, aiming to be Good Samaritans in the sense in which the Samaritan in Luke 10 takes care of the man who fell into the hands of the robbers. This, however, would require an attitude which

[22] Raunio 2001, 73, 89.
[23] LW 31, 41.

runs contrary to natural, egoistic, and desire-based human reasoning. According to Antti Raunio's interpretation of Luther, the Golden Rule looks away from loving good, beautiful, and pleasant people. It commands love to everyone, even to those who are the most difficult and unappealing. The Golden Rule demands a divine love that does not recognize existing goods but creates the goodness in its object.[24]

The Lutheran alternative to the "order of love" is thus nothing else than the perspective of God as giver. God's agape is God giving love to a world that is lacking it. Our rationalistic account of love is rather an evaluation of some already existing goodness. But this evaluation finally only reflects some self-interest. In Luther's account, Christians are called to imitate the divine love in such a manner that they fulfill the needs and wants of others. In that process, Christians become givers. One may note here that whereas the perspective of the creed considers human beings as receivers of God's act of giving, in the ethical-theological perspective of the Golden Rule the human being participates in the process of circulation and becomes, or at least is called to become, a giver.

Thus in Luther's analysis of human action there are two perspectives. First, there is the critical perspective in which all prudence is revealed to be egoism and in which even our love is shown to be a problematic evaluation in which we project our selfish value-hierarchies onto the world. Human beings cannot give true gifts on their own, since every gift is given in order to promote some self-interest and thus ceases to be a true gift.

Second, there is the perspective of God as poietic giver which becomes the model for interpreting the Golden Rule. This means giving gifts to enemies and regarding everybody as "you" whose needs we are called to meet. If the first and critical perspective is similar to Derrida's analysis, the second and positive side resembles Jean-Luc Marion's phenomenology of the gift. Probably for Luther, the positive perspective is not a rational account, but a spiritual account which is "given" in and through God's relationship to the world as the giver par excellence. Human reason on its own is a gift of God spoiled by pervasive egoism. Therefore it can only bring forth ambivalence and uncertainty. Only the spiritual gift can purify reason so that it can bring forth spiritual prudence and imitate the rule of divine love.

[24] UWC 107–8.

We have in this chapter outlined some general features of the theological tradition, exemplified by some New Testament writings, the Creed, and Martin Luther. In all these sources, giving occurs as a movement away from the giver, a movement which resembles but is not identical with the acts of sending and loving. The act of giving prompts circulation, since the receiver becomes a further giver. But this circulation should not blur the distinction between giver and receiver. The Father gives to the Son; the two divine persons are equal but asymmetric in the sense that the Son has received everything from the Father, and not vice versa. For Luther, a Christian should imitate the rule of God's outpouring, creative agape in order to circulate this love as the Golden Rule advises us. But this active moment of Christian love should not obscure the perspective that God is the giver, whereas humans are receivers.

We have already noted that some specific variants of giving, like the biblical *paradidômi*, need a more complex analysis, in which we add to the relationship among giver, gift and receiver a beneficiary, for whose sake something is given. The issue of self-giving, in which giver equals the gift, also proved to be a prominent biblical topic. In addition, there are variants of giving, self-giving, and handing over in which the giver and the receiver are "bracketed," that is, we are not directly told who they are. Still another dogmatically highly relevant topic is whether the "imitation" of God's giving is always the proper reaction of Christians. Can there be divine giving which we should not circulate but of which we remain only receivers and, perhaps, beneficiaries?

These open and complex matters will occupy us in the next chapters. Some of them deal with specific variants of giving, such as forgiving, thanksgiving, and sacrifice. They will be addressed in specific chapters. Others, for instance the issue of imitation and circulation, are broader topics which will be approached from various angles and summarized in the final chapters. Both the theological tradition presented here and the contemporary discussion described in the previous chapter provide us with the tools for further analysis.

As a final point one may note that we ended chapter 1 with John Milbank's idea of agape and this chapter with Luther's notion of God's love. These two are not in any clear agreement with each other. Luther probably could not call agape a "purified gift-exchange," since his interpretation of God's love is permeated by the fundamental distinction between the giver and the receiver. I have attempted to show that Luther is not completely unilateralist in his theology of love, since he admits the moments of reception and circulation. But he is probably much more unilateralist than Milbank. One could also say that Milbank is more "Augustinian" than Luther, at least in the sense that Luther's opposition to *ordo caritatis* and his insistence on "poietic" love separate him from Augustine's desire-based considerations. We have thus concluded this and the previous chapter with two different views of agape.

3

Forgiveness and Negative Giving

Forgiving and forgiveness are at the same time very simple and very complex theological phenomena. In religious education, asking and receiving forgiveness are among the first things that a child is supposed to learn. If you harm another person, you are supposed to say: "I'm sorry, I apologize." A child of five years normally understands this. Asking and receiving forgiveness is among the elementary truths of faith. Forgiveness of sins is included in the Apostles' Creed, in the Nicene Creed, and in the Lord's Prayer.

On the other hand, philosophers like Jacques Derrida ask whether ancient Greek culture, to which the creeds and the Lord's Prayer at least linguistically belong, knew an idea of forgiveness. And prominent New Testament scholars like Rudolf Bultmann conclude that forgiveness in the New Testament is "not strongly developed conceptually."[1] Reasons for these reservations can be found in the fact that the Greek verb that describes forgiving in the New Testament, *aphiêmi*, means literally "to send off," "to release," "to let be." The corresponding substantive, *aphesis*, "forgiveness," means release or liberation, for example, in Luke 4:18: "He [the Lord] has sent me to proclaim release (*aphesin*) to the captives and recovery of sight to the blind, to let the oppressed go free (*aphesei*), . . ."[2]

[1] Jacques Derrida, "To Forgive: The Unforgivable and the Imprescriptible," in *Questioning God* (= QG), eds., John D. Caputo, Mark Dooley, and Michael J. Scanlon (Bloomington: Indiana University Press, 2001) 21–51, here 22; Rudolf Bultmann, *aphiemi*, in *Theological Dictionary of the New Testament*, eds., Gerhard Kittel et al., abridged in one volume by Geoffrey Bromiley (Grand Rapids: Eerdmans, 1992) 88.

[2] In the following I will use, in addition to basic dictionaries, especially the excellent overview, with recent exegetical, theological and philosophical bibliographies by Adrian Schenker et al., "Vergebung der Sünden," in *Theologische Realenzyklopädie* 34 (2002) 663–91. I also draw from Hubert Frankemölle (ed.), *Sünde und Erlösung im Neuen Testament* (Freiburg: Herder, 1996).

Although forgiving and forgiveness are employed by the Synoptic Gospels in the religious sense that God forgives human sins and trespasses, one is left to wonder what this act of God is. Does it mean that God simply forgets the sins or generously looks away from them? Or does God in some way, economically or juridically, not "count" the sins of people in a heavenly book-keeping? Or is it meant that God liberates people from sin? Even in the act of release or liberation there seems to be no positive giving at stake, but only some obstacle is removed or annulled.

The Latin equivalents to the Greek word, employed both in the Vulgate and in especially in the liturgy, are *remitto* and *dimitto*. They have basically the same semantics as their Greek synonym. The classical dogmatic locus dealing with the forgiveness of sins is called in Latin *remissio peccatorum*. The Latin wording of the Lord's Prayer says: *dimitte nobis debita nostra* (Matt 6:12) or, in Luke 11:4, *peccata nostra*. These two "missions" of God in Latin likewise stress the "sending off" or even "sending back" of sins. In both Greek and Latin, the forgiver does not seem to give anything positive, but the act of granting forgiveness means rather taking away the existing problem either by looking away from it or by releasing or liberating the person from this problem.

This is curious because the vocabulary of many vernacular languages—"forgiveness" and "pardon" in English, *Vergebung* in German and *pardon* in French—suggests an act of positive giving, or even a gift (*don*). It seems that there is not only a "looking away from" or a release, but also some positive transfer of goodness at stake in the English word "forgiveness." This observation, among other things, lies behind Jacques Derrida's ruminations over the Greek way of speaking. Rudolf Bultmann's study perhaps indicates that we should not read too much later theology into the biblical concept.

Negative Giving: Kierkegaard and the New Testament

John Milbank has recently attended to this dichotomy between forgiveness as "negative gesture" and as "positive gift." Milbank describes the negative side as "forgetting" and as "negative giving." The latter for him comes close to Søren Kierkegaard's discussion of forgiveness as "de-creating," a process in which something ceases to exist.[3] We

---

[3] John Milbank, "Forgiveness: The Double Waters" (= FD), in his *Being Reconciled: Ontology and Pardon* (London: Routledge 2003) 44–60, here 44–45. Cf. also his "Forgiveness and Incarnation," in *QG*, 92–128.

may note in passing that already the scholastic theologians discussed the problem of "whether God can undo the past." In its literal meaning, the *remissio* of sacramental penance may give rise to the problem whether something is undone or de-created in the process of forgiving. A person who asks forgiveness is normally sorry for something that has happened in the past. Being sorry is an act of repentance. When forgiveness is granted, some past event becomes annulled or forgotten. Granting forgiveness therefore faces both an ethical and a philosophical problem. The ethical problem asks who has an authority, a moral right, and perhaps a duty to grant forgiveness. The philosophical problem asks what it means to act with regard to the past.

Milbank stresses that the linguistic point we have made concerning the Latin and Greek languages should not mean that the early Christians understood forgiveness in purely negative terms. Evil is something privative and negative, but God's forgiveness is a positive thing which involves not only ignorance or undoing, but also some positive gift. The vernacular languages underline this positive side in their renderings of the Latin terms. In the sacrament of penance, forgiveness should lead to recompense, restitution, and reconciliation. These are positive notions involving a creative act of something new, perhaps a gift. In addition to this, there is for Milbank another positive dimension to forgiveness. This is given by the atonement as an initial form of forgiveness. In the atonement, God is giving a gift on behalf of humankind. This first positive gift can be imitated in the interhuman acts of forgiveness, which on their part can cause "intersubjective contagion."[4]

In these ways forgiveness can be described in terms of giving and gift. The classical Christian notion of forgiveness includes both negative (forgetting, release) and positive (reconciliation, healing) elements. Although Milbank thinks that this synthesis has been broken since late medieval times, he claims that the classical notion is helpful in discussing contemporary problems related to forgiveness. The most difficult such problem concerns the extermination of the Jews in the Shoah. Is there any forgiveness available to the Nazis? Is it morally justified to forgive them?

For Jews to grant forgiveness for the Shoah to the Nazis would be absurd and perhaps also immoral. This has been argued forcefully by Vladimir Jankélévitch, according to whom "forgiveness died in the death camps." In his comment on Jankélévitch's work, Jacques Derrida

---

[4] FD 46.

points out that, on the one hand, this is morally true, since nothing can restore the wrongs of the Nazis. On the other hand, the very concept of forgiveness indicates something granted freely. We should not calculate or appeal to economic considerations in granting forgiveness, and it is possible and in some cases advisable to forgive somebody who does not ask for it or is already dead. Nevertheless, this last direction does not seem to work in the case of the Shoah. The Shoah cries for justice. The suffering of the Jews simply cannot be met adequately by any contemporary act of forgiveness.[5]

Derrida's comment belongs to a larger context in which he investigates the aporias of forgiveness. He points out that the concept of forgiveness entails philosophical problems that are similar to the issue of the gift.[6] As in the case of the gift, in my forgiving you for something, I increase my ethical status and place you in a doubtful role. It is a further problem whether the violated person has an obligation to forgive. Is it advisable to ascribe moral duties to the victim? A third group of problems emerges when the institution of forgiveness is presented in an economic fashion, in terms of balancing accounts. It can be argued, although the example is complex, that this has happened in the sacrament of penance. The acts of repentance and satisfaction repair the harm done. But if the person asking for forgiveness in a way pays for his past wrongs, can we speak of forgiving in the first place? Isn't it rather a compensation which takes place in such payment? As with the gift, generous giving becomes replaced by economic calculation.

Since we have dealt with such problems in chapter 1, I will now restrict my discussion of Derrida to the example of the Shoah and the challenges formulated by Jankélévitch. After investigating the conceptual problems, Derrida remarks that perhaps precisely because of such problems, forgiveness is often requested from God, for God may supersede the problems and apories of this concept.[7] For human beings, however, the problem remains: if you can compensate for the harm done or get an indemnity, forgiveness is strictly speaking not needed. But if you simply cannot compensate the harm done, asking and receiving forgiveness is reduced to lip service or it may be inadequate or even immoral, as in the case of the Shoah. Thus there is no real interhuman forgiveness, but either an interhuman compensation or the forgiveness which must be asked from God. It should again be noted that

[5] QG 7–8.
[6] QG 21–22.
[7] QG 44–46.

Derrida is not making a nihilist point, but he aims to show that we employ, and continue to employ, a notion whose very being we do not fully understand.

John Milbank is more optimistic with regard to a possible understanding of forgiveness. He suggests that the Augustinian account of the inseparability of time and memory can be helpful in this respect.[8] Milbank in fact thinks that the account given in Augustine's *Confessions* serves the purpose of clarifying the issue of divine forgiveness. For Augustine the past strictly speaking exists only in memory, which is the trace the past has left to us. As a finite and perishable thing, the past evil can absolutely fall away and be left only in the memory. Because of this ontological structure—time as memory and evil as privation—Milbank claims that Jankélévitch's resistance to forgiveness can be overcome. Milbank suggests that through re-narrating the past the memories can be healed. This does not mean complicity in the evil, but is a "correct refusal of the negative." The forgiver is not asked to give up his hatred to the wrongdoer, but through memory he can be led to a forgiving "dispossession of his own hatred."[9]

It is important to see how this result is reached by means of the Augustinian ontological commitments. Evil is finite and it can end, since past evil is given through memory. And since the process of healing occurs in memory, there is a path out of hatred and towards forgiveness. Milbank does not oversimplify the philosophical and ethical problems raised by Jankélévitch and Derrida. He points out that his is a necessarily theological vision. Moreover, Milbank wants to connect the Shoah with his view of forgiveness in order not to "glamourize" the Nazi crimes through rendering them outside of all explanation.[10] Thus he is doing more than Derrida and Jankélévitch. He gets this added value by adopting ontological premises from Augustine.

Milbank's distinction between the positive and the negative elements of forgiveness is helpful. This distinction allows us to see forgiveness not only as undoing or forgetting the past, but also as reconciliation and healing. Although the Greek and Latin concepts emphasize the negative side, the biblical material clearly connects these concepts with God's positive giving. In the New Testament it is in most cases God who finally grants forgiveness of sins, and these passages are embedded within a richer context of justification, reconciliation,

---

[8] FD 53–55.
[9] FD 54.
[10] FD 54–55.

and salvation. Biblical forgiveness belongs to the context of God's positive giving.

I think, however, that Milbank's ideas need further development to relate properly to the biblical and historical material. Connecting forgiveness with the rich content of atonement and salvation history is theologically necessary, but it does not lead to a clear and precise conceptual description of forgiveness. Drawing such a picture with the rigor and elaboration that are demanded by the complexity of the underlying phenomenon will be my aim in this chapter.

I will in the following defend the thesis that, in order to understand forgiveness in a clear and precise manner, we need two conceptual pairs which are independent of each other. The first pair is that of remembering and forgetting. These two internal acts or attitudes concern more or less all those involved in the process of forgiveness: the one who forgives, the one who is forgiven, and the victim. It is necessary to discuss in what sense forgiveness involves forgetting and remembering that which is forgiven. The first pair has to do with internal attitudes rather than with actions. As attitudes, remembering and forgetting are related to knowing and believing and, in the case of forgiveness, also to the attitude of mercy. What I call "attitude" is not just a mood, but a condition viewed as expressing a thought or feeling.

The other, and more complicated, conceptual pair is that of positive and negative giving. Giving has to with actions reaching out to the receiver rather than attitudes that may express a thought or feeling towards someone while nevertheless "remaining" in the subject. The main point of my thesis is that we can and should conceptualize and identify the phenomenon of "negative giving" in order to understand forgiveness properly. Furthermore, negative giving is not conceptually connected with forgetting. In this sense my approach differs from Milbank, who is concerned with the "double waters" of negative forgetting and positive remembrance. For Milbank, these two alternatives include all aspects of positive and negative forgiveness, whereas in my approach the dimension of positive and negative giving is conceptually independent of the dimension of remembering and forgetting. My approach will finally result in a cumulative notion of forgiveness in which we may distinguish among no less than four conceptual positions.

My approach is also an elaboration and a partial defense of Søren Kierkegaard's notion of forgiveness, which Milbank[11] criticizes for

---

[11] FD 45.

its understanding forgiveness as a negation. Milbank considers Kierkegaard's view to be a problematic heir of the Reformation, a remark which obviously prompts a Lutheran to react.

Let us begin with a brief presentation of Kierkegaard's idea. The Danish philosopher does not speak of negative giving, but he makes a brief point concerning God's forgiveness: "Forgetting, when God does it in relation to sin, is the opposite of creating, since to create is to bring forth from nothing, and to forget is to take back into nothing."[12] This point is compared with two conceptual pairs related to human forgiving. The first one is between faith and forgiveness: faith believes the unseen into what is seen, whereas forgiveness believes away what is seen. This is one of the strategies how "love hides a multitude of sins." Through an act of faith, the thing forgiven becomes forgotten. For Kierkegaard, the highest sense of this forgetting is "not the opposite of recollecting but of hoping." In hoping you think to give being, whereas in forgetting you think to take away being.[13]

What is at stake in this kind of human forgiveness is a "metaphor . . . invented by love." Perhaps God is really undoing the sin, but the human lover merely "hides" the sin or "believes away that which he indeed can see." Kierkegaard emphatically claims, however, that whereas ignorance removes nothing "from nature, . . . it is different with the relation of forgiveness to the multitude of sins; forgiveness takes the forgiven sin away."[14] Kierkegaard is thus very consciously proceeding on two different levels: there is the ontological model of divine creation and annihilation, a model which the loving believer applies to forgiveness. But there is also the model which proceeds on the level of attitudes: believing, hoping, forgetting, recollecting, loving.

On the one hand, the text presents the horizon of the loving believer as naïve illusion, but on the other hand, this horizon also receives surprising sympathy when, for example, the view "forgiveness neither subtracts or adds" is refuted. Kierkegaard claims that if somebody asks for forgiveness, the forgiver either increases the multitude of sins through his denial or decreases it through his pardon. Kierkegaard even says that a sin which is forgiven becomes smaller than the same sin without pardon. This is not merely an "optical illusion," but "actually so," since

[12] Søren Kierkegaard, *Works of Love* (= WL; Princeton: Princeton University Press, 1995) 296.
  [13] WL 295–96.
  [14] WL 294–96.

forgiveness "deprives the sin of life," whereas "to deny forgiveness provides the sin with sustenance."[15]

It is not adequate to build a rigid systematic account of this playful text. Kierkegaard's remarks provide us with a starting-point which is helpful insofar as it identifies the two dimensions, one of creating/adding vs. annihilating/subtracting, the other dealing with attitudes related to remembering and forgetting in human forgiveness. The two dimensions can be distinguished from each other even within their interplay.

We may here highlight another passage of *Works of Love* in which an even stronger distinction between external giving and internal attitude is made. This time Kierkegaard's sympathy lies with the latter. He remarkably defines the attitude of mercifulness as a work of love which "can give nothing and is able to do nothing." Nevertheless, it is this attitude which has primary importance. Kierkegaard observes that worldly talk about "generosity and charitable donations and gift upon gift is almost merciless." Christianity, however, is not about doing but essentially about mercifulness, an attitude which "has nothing to give." Mercifulness is something like openness, an attitude which exists independently of the external resources; it concerns the question of how: "how this everything and this nothing are done."[16]

This primacy of mercifulness will be important when we return to the dimension of attitudes underlying the act of forgiving. Before that we will, however, concentrate on the scale of "adding and subtracting." This dimension of creating and bringing back to nothing resembles the act of giving. In previous chapters we have only been concerned with positive giving and the poietic activity of God. In order to evaluate Kierkegaard and Milbank's claims, we have to ask some systematic questions which neither of them have posed. Is it at all meaningful to speak of negative giving as an alternative to positive giving? If it is, is negative giving something which only belongs to God, or are there acts of human negative giving? And finally, provided that we manage to outline such a concept, how does it relate to forgiveness? To these questions we will now turn.

When a gift is given, we speak of giving that is positive in the sense that the gift is added to the recipient. Let us now define "negative giving" as an act which fulfills the following three conditions. It is

[15] WL 296–97.
[16] WL 327–28.

(a) an act in which the giver acts on the recipient in such a manner that something is detracted or subtracted from the recipient. I do not mean, however, the act of taking in which the actor becomes a recipient, but an act through which the actor removes or "takes away" something from the recipient. In this sense (b) an act of negative giving takes away from the recipient, but the thing annihilated, reduced or removed is not transferred to the giver. (c) This act should in all other respects (for example, the purpose and the context of the act) resemble the act of positive giving. Thus the recipient should be a living person equipped with an openness to receive this act, she should see herself as receiver, and may even feel gratitude towards the giver. Let us call the features (a) through (c) the semantic conditions of negative giving.

Let us next consider the following examples: (1) a doctor gives a treatment to a patient. The doctor may remove a malignant tumor from the patient. Or he may keep the patient at a spa until the patient has learnt to eat less, to do more exercise, and has lost enough weight. There are many ways of "giving a medical treatment" in which nothing positive is given to the patient, but, on the contrary, the patient is loosing something: an illness, a tumor, or extra weight. As a result of "giving a treatment," the recipient loses something, but nothing is added to anyone else. Nevertheless, one can still say that the doctor is giving and the patient is receiving the treatment.

(2) A rich landowner of the Hellenistic age is using slave labor in order to accomplish the farm work. One day he decides to release the slaves. In giving the slaves their freedom, the landowner cancels his own right to have a payment for the release of each slave. In other words, the contract which gave him the right to own the slaves, is annulled. Literally, the landowner is giving nothing to the slaves, but only annulling the contract. This act of release or liberation is not a positive act of giving a gift. At least on the literal level, an impediment is removed when the slaves are released from the contract and the yoke of slavery. The act of annulling the existing contract thus fulfills the above-mentioned semantic conditions of negative giving.

(3) A person is in debt, but the creditor cancels the debt. Through annulling the debt, the creditor becomes a giver. The creditor is not, however, giving anything positive. Literally, he destroys the promissory note; and metaphorically, he lifts the burden from the indebted person. This act of negative giving resembles the release of slaves.

(4) The ruler gives amnesty to a prisoner. The ruler is literally giving no positive thing, but simply removing the sentence laid upon the

prisoner. Amnesty is by definition no act of commerce or calculative justice. It thus also fulfills the semantic conditions (a)–(c) of negative giving.

(5) The language of cleaning, cleansing, and purification resembles that of therapeutic treatment. An object or a person receives a treatment through which it, he, or she becomes clean or purified. Nothing is added to the recipient during this treatment, but something, such as dirt, is taken away. The person who gives the treatment is a giver, whereas the thing or the person cleansed is the recipient. As a result of this negative giving, the dirt is removed or taken away.

These five examples are less paradoxical than Kierkegaard's God. Nor do they represent any such Manichean dualism in which the dark side would be equal to positive being. With the help of these examples we can argue that many concrete acts fulfill the semantic conditions of negative giving. The examples are far from obvious, and we could discuss them extensively. In (2) and (3), one could claim that the acts of releasing the slaves and canceling the debt could also be formulated in terms of positive giving. In (1) and (5), one might object that therapy is rightly called therapy, and cleaning is rightly called cleaning. There is no real need to construct such a new phrase as negative giving. We could well do with expressions like "taking away."

We can grant these remarks but still claim that the phenomenon of negative giving receives some shape through these semantic conditions and examples. For two reasons, outlining such a phenomenon is helpful: first, it helps us to understand Kierkegaard's point that there is forgiveness which "subtracts" or "takes away." Second, and more importantly, this phenomenon helps us grasp the New Testament language of forgiveness.

Examples 1 to 5 describe the most important metaphorical meanings related to the verb *aphiêmi* and the substantive *aphesis* in the New Testament. "Metaphorical" here means simply the point of comparison, the context to which the concept is compared and from which it receives its meaning.[17] In Mark 2:3-15 Jesus is portrayed as a healer and physician, who forgives sins while healing the sick. In Acts 22:16 baptism is described as cleansing which washes away sins. In John 1:29, the Lamb of God "takes away" sin. In Luke 4:18, *aphesis* means release and liberation of the oppressed. The Lord's Prayer speaks of forgiving

---

[17] Both Schenker 2002, 668–78 and Frankemölle 1996, 18–52 employ this grouping of metaphors in order to highlight the biblical meaning of forgiveness. I use their results in the following discussion.

debts. Paul speaks frequently of how the law has lost its power since Christians are under the grace of Jesus Christ.

Exegetical studies emphasize that the New Testament concept of forgiveness is heavily influenced by its Jewish surroundings. In Judaism, God grants forgiveness of sins. At the same time, humans should be merciful to one another. This Jewish parallel between divine and human forgiveness is reflected in the Lord's Prayer: "And forgive us our debts, as we also have forgiven our debtors." Many other statements concerning forgiveness reflect some Old Testament usage. For these reasons, and because of different metaphorical contexts, exemplified by the five cases above, exegetical research has been reluctant to systematize the biblical notion of forgiveness in any rigid manner. On the contrary, it is normally emphasized that the biblical notion of forgiveness (of sins, normally granted by God, but also required in inter-human relations) receives its meaning from the context. This is also behind Bultmann's judgment that "though forgiveness is fundamental, it is not strongly developed conceptually." In view of these difficulties, the idea of God's "negative giving" as a core phenomenon around which forgiveness has developed, is helpful as a systematic construct. It provides the different metaphors of forgiveness with a common shape and connects forgiveness with other aspects of giving.

There is yet another biblical aspect which may connect the idea of negative giving with forgiveness. Derrida is supported by many theologians in the claim that forgiveness in the strictest sense is only possible for God. Protestant dogmatics and theological encyclopedias defend this view not only in terms of their content, but also in defining their theological entry not as forgiveness per se, but as "forgiveness of sins." It is not so much forgiveness as such, but God's forgiveness of sins which then becomes the theological issue. Protestant dogmatics sometimes has made a distinction that whereas God alone forgives sins, humans forgive each other the harm done.[18] Along the same line, the argument is sometimes made that in the New Testament sins are forgiven only by God and not by Jesus.[19] Although this is exaggerated, our concept of "negative giving" is illustrated through such modes of giving which are only possible for a giver who is situated high above the recipient, for example, a creditor, a slave-owner, or a healer.

[18] This is the position of *Theologische Realenzyklopädie*: Schenker 2002, 683.
[19] A defense of this view, problematic in light of Mark 2:5 and Matt 9:6, is given e.g., in Frankemölle 1996, 86.

Divine and Human Forgiveness

The approach which restricts forgiveness of sins to God faces the following problem: The New Testament applies the Jewish idea that forgiveness among human beings should accompany or even precede God's forgiveness of sins. Biblical material is difficult in this respect, since sometimes it is indicated that only God can forgive sins, as the scribes claim in Mark 2:7. But sometimes, as in Matthew 18:22, one should forgive one's neighbor seventy-seven times. Even if the forgiveness of sins in the strict and final sense would belong to God, there should be some continuity between human and divine forgiveness. The Lord's Prayer, and especially its addition in Matthew 6:14-15, is the classical example of this continuity. God's "taking away" should be accompanied or even preceded by human forgiveness

Is it possible for me to grant forgiveness to "my debtors" through some act of negative giving? Perhaps it is, but only in some quite modest sense. Concerning the examples 1–5 above, the problem is that the person granting forgiveness should be a more powerful person than its recipient. Although the examples are taken from interhuman relations, they serve better as illustrations of divine forgiveness. But forgiveness between equals does not seem to work at the "ontological" level of positive and negative giving. At the ontological level such exchange becomes an economic transaction or some other form of compensation, not forgiveness, as Derrida and others have pointed out.

In the New Testament, interhuman forgiveness often takes the form of our example (3), financial debt. The parallel between divine and interhuman forgiveness is to some extent described in Matthew 18:23-35, in which the king settles accounts with his servants. Jesus teaches that the one who is forgiven a debt should have mercy on others. As in the Lord's Prayer, interhuman forgiveness is presented as a condition of divine forgiveness. One way of reading this story is to say that the creditor should exercise the virtue of generosity. Forgiving your debtors would thus be an act of generosity. A problem of this understanding of human forgiveness is, however, that it applies to cases in which the forgiver is not precisely a victim, but a creditor who still has the upper hand over the debtor. Furthermore, human generosity as a notion related to positive and negative giving is strongly economic. If a generous person covers another person's debt, this is not necessarily an act of forgiveness, but an act of benevolent charity. We earlier quoted Kierkegaard saying that human generosity is "almost merciless."

In order to grasp human forgiveness and its relationship to God's forgiveness of sins, we need the other basic dimension, the attitude-based scale of remembering and forgetting. With its help we may grasp the metaphorical nature of biblical narratives of forgiveness in relation to human forgiveness. In speaking of God, the negative giving expressed by our examples 1–5 illustrates the ontological act of God who annuls, undoes, or takes away our sin. In speaking of human beings, the ontological act in question remains an act of concrete giving. Of course, the literal reading is important: forgiving debts must mean forgiving real and concrete debts. But, in order to highlight something more general than economic ethics, we probably need an interpretation in which human forgiveness is not primarily an act reaching out to the receiver, but a specific attitude underlying the concrete act.

A biblical way of arguing for this dimension of attitudes proceeds from the close relationship between forgiveness and metanoia, repentance or change of mind. As a human attitude, forgiveness can be characterized as a change of mind towards mercy. Mark 1 and 2 show this relationship with regard to the human reception of forgiveness, John the Baptist proclaims "a baptism of *metanoia* for the forgiveness of sins" (1:4). After this, Jesus proclaims *metanoia* (1:14) and starts to forgive sins (2:5-10). The Sermon on the Mount (Matt 5–7), which is the context of the Lord's Prayer and especially of linking interhuman and divine forgiveness (Matt 6:14-15), emphasizes everywhere that human attitude of mercy which results from a fundamental change of mind.

What God requires from humans is thus not in the first place an ontological act of negative giving, but an attitude of mercy towards neighbors. God's forgiveness operates within both dimensions of mercy and of effective giving, whereas human forgiveness operates primarily within the boundaries of mercy. Humans can and sometimes they should give, but an external human act of forgiveness almost inevitably becomes a compensation or a liaison, just as a human gift creates indebtedness and dependencies. Therefore it is the internal attitude of mercy which is emphasized in human forgiveness.

With this result, we still have some problems with Kierkegaard's position. He claims emphatically in the concluding part of *Works of Love* that "God forgives you neither more nor less nor otherwise than as you forgive those who have sinned against you."[20] This reflects his almost heroic understanding of human forgiveness as an act which is

---

[20] WL 380.

capable of reducing the multitude of sin. Insofar as the attitude of mercy, or Kierkegaard's mercifulness, is concerned, our result is probably compatible with his opinion. As an attitude which, as Kierkegaard says, "has nothing to give,"[21] mercy can operate on that scale of forgiveness that concerns attitudes, such as forgetting and re-membering. Through this internal scale of mercy, humans are called to a conformity with God. But our focus on the ontological scale of giving yields the result that God forgives sins "more" and "otherwise" than we do. God's forgiveness proceeds "otherwise" than forgiveness among equals. Kierkegaard's claim can be read as an exhortation for us to deepen our understanding of human forgiveness, but this very deep-ening must lead into a partial refutation of his claim.

It can thus be argued that the essential parallelism between human and divine forgiveness concerns in the first place the attitude of mercy. Humans simply cannot abolish or forgive sins in the way God does. What is possible for us is an attitude of mercy that, it must be em-phasized, ought to be accompanied with external works of love, be-nevolence, generosity, and charity. But these human acts of positive and sometimes perhaps also negative giving do not accomplish the forgiveness of sins in any strict sense. They remain in the sphere of eco-nomic exchange and compensation, whereas forgiveness of sins in the strict sense is reserved to God. The parallel required by the Lord's Prayer as well as by many similar Jewish sources is concerned with our *metanoia* and mercy.

With this move it is not my intention, however, to downplay the dimension of attitudes, of remembering and forgetting, believing and mercy. This dimension is probably as essential for the understanding of forgiveness as the other dimension of negative and positive giving. I share the view of Kierkegaard that mercy is more fundamental for hu-mans than external giving. In the attitude-based scale of remembering and forgetting, human persons appear not only as recipients, but also as producers of forgiveness. Mercy is an attitude which can be directed towards another person. Concerning this scale, my position comes close to Milbank and other such writers who stress the need to have both positive remembrance and negative forgetting. Practical work to-wards reconciliation and peace by means of "truth commissions" and other such co-operative instruments has clearly shown that positive re-membrance and an even painful healing of memories are vitally im-

[21] WL 317.

portant when we aim at reaching an attitude of mercy and a forgiveness among equals.[22]

Since in my discussion the other scale, that of positive and negative giving, takes care of the "ontological" dimension of forgiveness, I do not see why we should adopt an Augustinian view of memory in order to understand forgiveness properly. There might be other reasons for adopting it, since it is a comprehensive and impressive vision of time, mind, and history, but we do not need it to understand biblical forgiveness or most Christian theologies of mercy and reconciliation.

My emphasis on negative giving should not mean either that the positive giving of God is downplayed. Since God's positive giving is extensively discussed in other chapters of this book, there is no urgent need to treat it here in detail. One obvious question should nevertheless be addressed: You claim that God's forgiveness of sins can be described in terms of negative giving. In addition, you claim that divine and human forgiveness comprise the attitude of mercy and that this attitude should include both remembrance and forgetting. Given this, how does God's positive giving relate to forgiveness? Is it as necessary in the scale of giving as the positive remembrance in the scale of attitude?

A brief answer is: Yes, in the sense that the positive gift belongs to God's action towards human beings, as many chapters of this book show. But we do not call God's positive gifts normally "forgiveness of sins." They are the gifts of grace, salvation or sacramental reality, union with Christ, sanctification, and so on. Although forgiveness is accompanied with the positive gifts in the sense that both of these are given through preaching, worship, and the rites of the church, it is useful to make a conceptual distinction between "God's forgiveness of sins" and the positive gifts. This distinction has been attempted above through the construct of God's "negative giving" as it becomes expressed in many important New Testament metaphors of forgiveness. There certainly is a fundamental link between forgiveness and other gifts in that they all display the dynamics of giving and gift. The distinction between "positive" and "negative" giving is, therefore, finally a relative distinction within the totality of God's giving and gifts. It has been employed in order to describe in what sense forgiveness, in spite of Greek and Latin etymologies, displays the logic of divine giving.

---

[22] See e.g., R. Scott Appleby, "Reconciliation and the Politics of Forgiveness," in his *The Ambivalence of the Sacred* (New York: Rowman & Littlefield, 2000) 167–204.

The question is, however, quite complex. John Milbank argues that "the prime paradigm for positive forgiveness is the Incarnation and Atonement."[23] My discussion of forgiveness is more restrictive. It does not try to relate the whole theology of atonement and incarnation to forgiveness, but remains at the conceptual level. In exegetical and dogmatic literature, forgiveness is related to almost every other important biblical concept, and not without some reason. My strategy has been to concentrate on forgiveness in order to give this concept a clearer shape. I am ready to admit that a more comprehensive range of God's gifts becomes prominent when we move from negative to positive giving. That they take other conceptual and theological forms does not mean that they would be unrelated to forgiveness.

There is perhaps one rather concrete way to show in what sense our description of forgiveness, focussed on the two dimensions, can be helpful in concrete church life, and especially in the ecumenical discussion. Remembering and forgetting, positive and negative giving do not exclude each other in any way. On the contrary, they are probably all needed in order to understand the various shapes of divine and human forgiveness. Still, there is probably a human tendency to play remembering against forgetting, and to play positive gifts against negative giving. The Nazi crimes discussed above offer a prominent example of the difficult interplay between remembering and forgetting. Within this interplay, one may argue that either one, taken alone, is inadequate, and that they logically exclude one another. Concerning positive and negative giving, one might ask a parallel difficult question as follows: is God's giving "nutritive" in the sense that God pours the plentiful gifts over us, or rather "ascetic" in the sense that we are laid bare and released from dependencies on the world around us? This difficult interplay is related to the old question of whether God educates Christians through success or through the cross.

If these two dimensions manifest two different interactions, then we obtain, with some simplification of the issues, a fourfold typology of emphases related to forgiveness:

(1) negative giving—forgetting: God abolishes sin and we, too, are merciful to our neighbors and need not remember past harms.

(2) negative and positive giving—forgetting: God not only abolishes sin but also gives us abundant gifts. We are merciful and can for-

get the sin. Thus, with the help of God, we can start a new life in which God's gifts are poured upon us.

(3) negative giving—forgetting and remembering: God takes away the sin of the world. We are called to merciful forgetting, but at the same time we should remember our sin and live in the consciousness of it.

(4) negative and positive giving—forgetting and remembering: God takes away the sin and heals the world with gifts. We are called to be merciful and to forget each other's trespasses. At the same time, we are called to remember and discuss even the painful memories openly. This reminds us of our sin, but at the same time it can lead, prompted through God's positive gifts, to a healing of these memories.

Although these four positions are caricatures, they have some heuristic value in an attempt to define how different Christian churches think about forgiveness. The first position, consisting of negative giving and forgetting, is more or less a common starting-point approved by all denominations. The second position, which connects forgetting with both negative and positive giving, resembles some naive versions of born-again Protestantism, but perhaps also some naïve versions of such Roman Catholicism in which the sacrament of penance works mechanically or provides an automatic healing. Leaving sins behind while embracing positive sanctification becomes problematic because the positive remembrance is not taken seriously. The second position may therefore be unable to provide lasting reconciliation.

The third position comes close to Lutheranism and its proclamation of the Christian who is "justified and sinner at the same time." An awareness of the sins is not lost, although it is sincerely believed that sins are forgiven. Thus there is a balance between remembrance and forgetting. God's giving is seen primarily in terms of "negative giving." Christians are educated through hardships and even tribulation. God remains *Deus absconditus*, a hidden God. One may even say that God's negative giving is not limited to forgiveness, but plays a broader role in the Christian's life under the cross. For Martin Luther, a true theologian "comprehends the visible and manifest things of God seen through suffering and the cross."[24] Because of this emphasis, adherents of the third position often give a restricted picture of the positive healing power of the sacraments and are suspicious of charismatic theology.

---

[24] Luther, Heidelberg Disputation, thesis 20. In *Luther's Works*, American Edition, vol. 31 (St. Louis: Concordia, 1957) 40.

Extreme forms of a "theology of the cross" may run the risk of loosing the perspective that God is as merciful in negative as in positive giving.

The fourth position is the most saturated view of forgiveness, since it pays attention to all dimensions. While sins are forgiven, we need to work towards a conscious healing of memories. God abolishes sin and gives the good gifts which we can enjoy and put into use. If the fourth position is nevertheless also aware of the starting-point of forgiveness (first position), it is an ideal understanding of forgiveness. If this origin is lost, however, the fourth position may be in danger of becoming too anthropocentric. An activist who incessantly speaks of the Shoah and other crimes against humanity, while feeling strongly empowered by God in doing such, may be an example of an exaggerated understanding of forgiveness as positive and under our control. As an ideal model, the fourth position probably requires a less strenuous view of the human person who needs to be merciful not only because it is an ethical duty, but fundamentally because God's giving and forgiving is still the fundamental reality towards which human *metanoia* turns.

This fourfold division is not only a mapping of different denominational attitudes towards forgiving, but also an outline of the cumulative reality of forgiveness. When forgiveness proceeds from negative giving and forgetting to remembrance and positive gifts, our understanding of it grows and in some sense becomes more mature. In this way the model agrees with John Milbank's insistence on the need for a more positive notion of forgiveness which includes remembrance and reconciliation.

At the same time, however, the model very consciously aims at preserving the Lutheran affinity towards negative giving and towards the being of a Christian as "sinner and justified." Although the way from (1) to (4) proceeds in a cumulative fashion, it is not meant that the starting-point (1) would be inadequate or that it lacks something truly fundamental. The core meaning of *aphesis* and *aphiêmi* is preserved when forgiveness is understood as God's merciful negative giving and as that mercy among equals that overlooks the debts and trespasses of one's neighbor seventy-seven times. The starting-point (1) may be less developed than the other forms (2,3,4), but at the same time it is also more unproblematic than the developed variants of forgiveness.

It must again be emphasized that this model does not embrace Milbank's Augustinian ontology in which the negative and the privative stand for evil, while the positive is connected with goodness. I share Kierkegaard's rather Lutheran idea that God can act through negative giving. God's annihilating work is certainly not evil, but it is as merciful as God's positive giving. God can act for the good of humans through both creative and privative giving, through both nourishing and ascetic paths of life. God can act through connecting us with something, but also through releasing us from something else. On the other hand, our view of negative giving does not amount to any reification of the negative, since concepts like releasing and liberation are not dualistic.

Although the core meaning of forgiveness is in this model defined with the help of negative giving, I do think with Milbank that we must broaden the concept towards positive meanings, through which some transfer of goodness, a reconciliation or healing, can occur. This is necessary in order to face the above-mentioned problems posed by Jankélévitch and Derrida. Their examples show that the core meaning of forgiveness is alone insufficient to meet the aporia of interhuman evil. I am not claiming, however, that the model outlined here could really explain these apories. Whereas Milbank with his Augustinian model seeks to give explanations even with regard to the Shoah, my discussion rather strengthens the observation of Derrida that forgiveness is perhaps "reserved for God."[25]

Søren Kierkegaard's heroic, but also to an extent ironic, attempt to see human forgiveness as a "work of love" which does away with the sin of our loved ones, approaches the poietic love of God in a truly Lutheran manner. But he pays a high price for doing this: the person whose love in extreme good faith hides the sins of the beloved appears ridiculous and caught in illusion. A strict, ontological forgiveness of sin requires a giver who is high above the person in need of forgiveness. A loving human person who hides his neighbor's sins behind his own back, appears to be a megalomaniac, since he is not above the neighbors. Even less can or should a victim forgive the wrongdoer's sins in this manner.

Forgiveness among equals works in a more modest and more attitude-based manner. Often it only works very slowly and even then mercy and *metanoia* must be complemented with ontological and economic strategies of compensation and sometimes punishment. In addition to the strict and theocentric core meaning of forgiveness, the fourfold model highly recommends interhuman strategies of

---

[25] QG 44.

reconciliation and positive remembrance, exemplified in particular by positions (3) and (4). They cannot "take away the sins of the world," but they may provide education and healing, ascetic and nourishing strategies for equipping people to deal with wrongs done in the past.[26]

What is the relevance of this rather elaborate theory of forgiveness for ecumenism? We may explore this question through looking briefly at the section "Justification as forgiveness of sins and making right-eous" in the Lutheran—Roman Catholic *Joint Declaration on the Doctrine of Justification*.[27] In this section, "forgiveness of sins" is employed as a shorthand for God's declaratory act by which "God no longer imputes to them their sin." This way of speaking is traditionally Lutheran. It employs the forensic metaphor of amnesty and, to a lesser extent, the economic metaphor of debt. God's forgiving love is called by Lutherans traditionally "the favor of God," an attitude resulting from God's mercy and the forgiveness of sins.[28]

The Lutheran understanding is thus characterized by God's nega-tive giving (metaphors 3 and 4 above) and by the attitude of God's favor, a condition of thought by which sin is both remembered (the person remains a sinner) and forgotten (the person is declared right-eous). Together these yield the position 3 in our classification. The ecu-menical problem related to this position is whether it allows for the idea of "making righteous." Catholics emphasize "the renewal of the interior person through the reception of grace imparted as a gift to the believer"[29] and thus they clearly want to embrace the position 4 of our classification. But are the Lutherans willing to take the step from 3 to 4?

According to the section, this is indeed the case. Lutherans do not "deny the renewal of the Christian's life." What they want to stress is that "only in union with Christ is one's life renewed."[30] In this sense Luther-ans want to emphasize that embracing the most saturated position 4 should not lead into an anthropocentric positive control of forgiveness. The connection with the starting-point of forgiveness must be taken seri-ously. Catholics on their part are ready to say that they do not "deny that God's gift of justification remains independent of human cooperation."

---

[26] Appleby 2000 presents an overview of such strategies among Christians, but also among other people of good will.

[27] Joint Declaration on the Doctrine of Justification (= JD), 1999, §22–24, in *Growth in Agreement* vol. 2, eds., Harding Meyer et al. (Grand Rapids: Eerdmans, 2000) 569–70.

[28] JD 22–23.

[29] JD 24.

[30] JD 23.

We see that our classification helps us to understand the dynamics of this ecumenical text. I would nevertheless add that the traditional Lutheran way of speaking of forgiveness as an amnesty and a favor is, in view of our classification, too narrow. The theocentric focus implied by these notions did effectively correct some misdevelopments in the sixteenth century, but the notions of amnesty and favor simply do not carry the whole meaning of forgiveness. Precisely for this reason the forensic side is complemented by the idea of "making righteous," that is, the idea of "the gift of new life in Christ."[31] The whole section repeats several times that these two aspects of God's gracious action are simultaneous and cannot be separated.

We may fully agree with this repeated emphasis, but we can also add a last critical remark: given all this, why are the two aspects given in Lutheranism the distinct names of favor and gift, since forgiveness can be comprehensively understood in terms of giving and gift? A conceptual distinction can be drawn between God's mercy and God's gift even in their concrete togetherness, but forgiveness and gift participate in one another both in reality and at the conceptual level.

[31] JD 22.

4

Sacrifice and Thanksgiving

Like forgiveness, sacrifice is a topic relevant not only for theology, but also for philosophy and the study of human cultures. The contemporary cultural relevance of forgiveness, as we have seen, lies in the Nazi crimes of the Second World War, but also in political issues related to the work of "truth commissions" in South Africa and elsewhere. The contemporary discussion of sacrifice has a similar but larger cultural background. Sacrifice becomes easily related to violence and bloodshed, and it can be asked whether religions that emphasize sacrifice and martyrdom rather promote violence than act as peacemakers.[1]

In this chapter, however, I will not focus on the general issue of religion and violence. Instead, I aim at reaching some conceptual clarity on the meaning of sacrifice in religion, especially in relation to discussions within and between some Christian churches. As a dogmatic topic, sacrifice relates primarily to the death of Jesus and its theological interpretation as satisfaction or redemption. As an ecumenical topic, sacrifice is mostly discussed in the context of the sacrament of the altar, the Eucharist. In order to understand the Reformation criticism of Roman Catholicism, conceptual clarity is needed about both the Eucharist and its relationship to the death of Jesus. At the same time, the broader cultural background of "religion and violence" should not

[1] See e.g., Leo D. Lefebure, *Revelation, the Religions and Violence* (Maryknoll, N.Y.: Orbis, 2000), and Hent de Vries, *Religion and Violence: Philosophical Perspectives from Kant to Derrida* (Baltimore: Johns Hopkins University Press, 2002). De Vries contains much material on sacrifice.

simply be forgotten. We will discuss in what sense this broader issue is relevant even concerning the specific issue of the Eucharist.

Like forgiveness (ch. 3), sacrifice is at the same time a very common and a very difficult phenomenon. It is common to many, if not most, religions and it has played a prominent role in archaic cultures. On the other hand, scholars debate what this role and the meaning of sacrifice has been. There are many anthropological theories of sacrifice, but none of them has gained universal acceptance.[2] In this broad cultural sense, anthropological theories are not very helpful in explaining the ecumenical problems related to the eucharistic sacrifice.

The Augustinian–Thomistic Grammar of Sacrifice

In classical theology since Augustine, there exists a remarkable conceptual clarity regarding sacrifice. In *De trinitate* 4,3,19 Augustine states: "Now there are four things to be considered in every sacrifice: to whom it is offered, by whom it is offered, what it is that is offered, and for whom it is offered." This fourfold distinction remains the standard tool of analysis in Western theology. Thomas Aquinas quotes it in *Summa theologiae* (Sth) III, q22, a3, ad1 as well as in q48 a3 c. Wolfgang Simon has shown the relevance of this four-place relation for the theological understanding of sacrifice.[3] We have already employed a parallel model in earlier chapters with regard to the act of giving, which requires (1) the giver, (2) the gift and (3) the receiver. As we noted in chapter 3, some acts of giving also presuppose (4) a beneficiary for whose sake something is given. Sacrifice is normally characterized by the very fact that there is a beneficiary for whose sake the offering takes place.

We can immediately note, however, that Augustine's fourfold division of sacrifice is a syntactic description which does not characterize the content of sacrifice. Thomas Aquinas distinguishes among sacrifices, offerings, and tithes (Sth II/2 85 a3 ad3) as different acts in which something is offered by humans. In both sacrifices and offerings, the receiver is God, but sacrifices are those offerings in which something

---

[2] See e.g., Peter Gerlitz, et al., "Opfer" in *Theologische Realenzyklopädie 25*, 253–99 (with excellent bibliographies of English and German literature up to 1995); *Das Opfer: Biblischer Anspruch und liturgische Gestalt*, eds., Albert Gerhards und Klemens Richter (Freiburg: Herder, 2000).

[3] Wolfgang Simon, *Die Messopfertheologie Martin Luthers* (Tübingen: Mohr Siebeck, 2003). Simon reviews also contemporary anthropological and philosophical literature.

"sacred" is done to the gift. Thus for Thomas, the notion of sacrifice is defined through its being offered to God in a manner which sanctifies or transforms the gift. Thomas follows Augustine in saying that only offerings to God can be called sacrifices in the proper sense (Sth II/2 q85 a2, *De civ. Dei* 10,4-6)

Thomas's account has in many ways remained plausible. If I donate money for some good purpose, my donation can be called an offering in which the four locations within the relation are relevant. Likewise, if I pray for you, I give God a metaphorical gift and you become the beneficiary. But we do not call these acts sacrifices, even though we may understand in what sense tithing or intercession resembles sacrifice. Thus the fourfold description is a necessary but by no means sufficient characterization of the phenomenon of sacrifice. Within the limits of this chapter, we do not aim at reaching a sufficient characterization of the extremely complex topic of sacrifice, but will limit our discussion to this observation of a parallel between sacrifices and other acts of giving.

It is important to realize that sacrifice is understood in classical theology in terms of giving a gift. The Latin verb *offerre* employed in this context denotes the act of giving a gift. In this offering a human giver offers a gift to God for someone's benefit. This four-place relation is also how formal characteristics of the eucharistic sacrifice were fundamentally understood in the medieval canon of the Mass.[4] Thomas Aquinas describes the Eucharist as follows: "This sacrament is both a sacrifice and a sacrament. It has the nature of a sacrifice in that it is offered, and of a sacrament in that it is received. Therefore, its effect as a sacrament is in the recipient, its effect as a sacrifice is in the offerer or in those for whom it is offered" (Sth III q79 a5 r).

From this quotation, we see the two senses of the eucharistic gift. Within the general logic of the gift, the human receiver (3) enjoys the good contained in the sacramental gift (2). In addition, there is a specific sacrificial logic which concerns the priest as offerer (1), God as receiver (3) and Christians as beneficiaries (4). Within this logic, many say that the gift to God covers some debt of the beneficiaries. Before entering this logic of compensation or "satisfaction," we must first note that sacrifice is for Thomas one of the acts by which humans worship God through offering to God something external to God (Sth II/2 q85).

[4] Simon 2003, 132.

Thus in the eucharistic sacrifice the priest occupies position (1) in the fourfold relation. He offers the Eucharist to God in order that humans may benefit from this sacrifice. Thomas says (Sth III q79 a5r) that the Eucharist "becomes a satisfaction for them for whom it is offered, or even for the offerers, according to the measure of their devotion." He points out that the sacrament of the Eucharist was not instituted for satisfaction but for spiritual nourishment. But, since this nourishment also is an effect of charity "from the fervor of which man obtains forgiveness," the eucharistic sacrifice may to some extent have a power of satisfaction for the devoted beneficiaries of the eucharistic sacrifice.

Given this, how does the eucharistic sacrifice relate to forgiveness and satisfaction? Sacrifice and satisfaction in the Eucharist are connected with the passion of Christ which is the true sacrifice and obtains sufficient satisfaction (Sth III q48 a3, a4c). In the relationship between Christ's sacrifice on the cross and the eucharistic sacrifice it is therefore important to explain both the moment of difference and that of identity. The difference is visible in the classical claim that Christ's death on the cross was *ephapax* (Heb 10:10), a unique, perfect, and sufficient sacrifice that brought about complete satisfaction. The Mass does not add anything to the value of Christ's unique and complete sacrifice. In this sense the two are completely different.

But there is also a moment of identity which can be described in temporal terms, as memory, or in iconic terms, as representation. The eucharistic sacrifice in some way represents the sacrifice of Christ and is done in remembrance of Christ's passion. Memory and representation thus connect the eucharistic sacrifice to Christ's work of satisfaction on the cross.[5]

Taking into account this emphasis on both difference and identity, one can understand Thomas as saying that forgiveness is fundamentally obtained through Christ's work of satisfaction. The eucharistic sacrifice can, however, create a devotion, a spirit of *metanoia* which is needed in order to attain forgiveness, as we observed in chapter 3. In this sense the Eucharist is also a channel of satisfaction. We are here not so much concerned with the general plausibility of Thomas's doctrine as with his use of the two perspectives: the sacramental logic of the gift and the concomitant logic of sacrifice. Because he presupposes the four relational places in discussing sacrifice, he can distinguish between the

[5] Simon 2003, 20–39.

sacramental nourishment of the human receiver (3) and the sacrificial devotion of the offerer (1) and the beneficiaries (4).

The conceptual distinction among the four locations within the relation does not mean, of course, that all placeholders were really distinct from each other. In Christ's sacrificial self-giving (Sth III q48 a3), the giver and the gift are identical. As we saw in chapter 3 and as is normally the case in the eucharistic sacrifice, the receiver of the gift may also be among the beneficiaries. The four-place grammar probably nevertheless excludes some identifications among the places. Normally the giver is distinct from receiver. Moreover, one cannot be both the gift and the beneficiary, since the beneficiary is supposed to lack something that the gift contains. Even these oppositions, however, can be challenged. Augustine offers an extreme identification among the different places of the sacrificial relation. After introducing "the four things to be considered in every sacrifice," he says that in Jesus Christ all four places become one: "This one true mediator, in reconciling us to God by his sacrifice of peace, would remain one with him to whom (3) he offered it, and make one in himself those for whom (4) he offered it, and be himself who (1) offered it one and the same as what (2) he offered" (*De trin.* 4,3,19).

This condensed picture is elaborated in various ways in post-Augustinian sacrificial theology. One important moment of this elaboration becomes visible in the claim that sacrifice is a human act of giving something external to God. If this is taken literally, then the death of Christ on the cross can only be a sacrifice if it is described as the human person Jesus giving himself to God. It doesn't make sense to say that those who crucified Jesus were themselves bringing about satisfaction. But since sacrifice is by definition an act that a human being performs in relation to God, Jesus Christ in his humanity had to give himself to death and to God.

Augustine's and Thomas's definition of sacrifice as a holy act performed by human beings to God also establishes another important moment of this theological grammar of sacrifice. Since only God can occupy the place of the receiver (3), many complicated biblical and dogmatic issues are given a preliminary answer. If the New Testament notion of *paradidômi*, handing over or delivery (ch. 2) is employed within a sacrificial context, normally in a biblical passage in which a beneficiary is mentioned, it can only mean that something is given to God. The death of Christ as a sacrifice must therefore be an act in which Christ becomes, theologically speaking, handed over to God.

The satisfaction obtained through the sacrifice on the cross thus concerns our debt to God, not to Satan or to death. Parallel to this, the eucharistic sacrifice must conceptually be an act in which the priest gives something to God. This theological grammar gives us in fact a variety of acts in which humans offer something to God and by so doing benefit others. Obviously, this way of speaking creates both opportunities and problems.

Given that in the Augustinian-Thomistic grammar of sacrifice a human being gives (1) something to God (3), one can interpret the benefit (4) achieved as a counter-gift, a favor which God grants to a group of humans. Normally, this group of beneficiaries is not identical with the original giver. An intercessory prayer, for instance, is offered to God in order that someone else is healed or given peace by God. The self-giving act of the human-divine person Jesus Christ on the cross was offered to God for the salvation of many. Since the benefit achieved in this way does not concern the original giver, it is not a counter-gift in any strict sense. It nevertheless to some extent resembles a counter-gift.

Certain classical dogmatic problems are related to the claim that in Christianity human beings offer sacrifice to God. For many modern theologians, this claim creates problems. Although I sympathize with them in various ways, I will in the following argue that this claim may also alleviate some problems. In particular, I will argue that God appears less violent if we consistently think of sacrifices as human and not as divine acts. We will first look at this argument more closely. After that, we will analyze in more detail the question of eucharistic sacrifice. When we in the following treat these two topics successively, it is important to remember their connection with the "Augustinian-Thomistic grammar of sacrifice," a view which proceeds from presupposing the human being as giver and God as receiver.

Religion and Violence: Anselm of Canterbury and René Girard

Various theories of atonement, in particular Anselm of Canterbury's view of satisfaction offered to God through the death of Jesus, face the problem of underlying violence. Since the Enlightenment, Christianity has been criticized for its emphasis on the blood of Christ which allegedly must be shed in order to bring satisfaction to God. Our sinfulness has caused a debt to God and a defamation of God's glory. Since humankind is incapable of rehabilitation and compensation,

Jesus Christ offers to bring these about through his vicarious death which effects satisfaction. This description of atonement seems to presuppose a view of God who needs violence and even bloodshed in order to become appeased. Some theologians have simply affirmed that this is the case, whereas others have attempted to construct theories of atonement which would be nonviolent in their basic outlook.[6]

Although Anselm's theory enjoys a certain prominence in Western theology, the Christian churches have not limited their language of reconciliation, atonement, and salvation to any one dogmatic theory. Therefore there is room to develop or at least modify the existing historical theories of atonement. We will not enter this discussion as such, since it is complex and must attend to various dimensions of theology. But our limited perspective of "giving" and "sacrifice" may be helpful in dealing with some problems of the Anselmian view.

In *Cur deus homo*, Anselm outlines a theory of redemption. Some aspects of his discussion resemble the Augustinian-Thomistic grammar of sacrifice. When Anselm speaks of the humanity of Christ, he points out that a human person "ought to do" (*nec facere illam debet nisi homo, Cur deus homo* II, 6) the satisfaction to God. The logic behind this "ought to" is complex, but basically it means that the act of satisfaction should be performed by one of the debtors to qualify as a compensation. Only God, however, has the power to perform such an act. Therefore Christ had to be God-man.[7]

Without discussing the validity of Anselm's whole argument, we see that Anselm emphasizes the role of the human person as the one who gives compensation. The human person must occupy the position of the agent (*facere debet homo*) in order that humans can be redeemed. It is probably an exaggeration to call this an "anthropocentric" moment of Anselm's theory of satisfaction, but he clearly presents the view that humans cannot be mere spectators of this event. A human person must occupy the position of the "doer" or "giver" in order that accounts become even. Moreover, this compensation is not paid to Satan. Anselm rejects the so-called "devil-ransom theory" ascribed to Augustine. It is the dishonor done to God which needs satisfaction; the compensation is thus given to God.

---

[6] For the post-Enlightenment discussion, cf. J. Denny Weaver, *The Nonviolent Atonement* (Grand Rapids: Eerdmans, 2001); Ingolf Dalferth, "Die Heilsbedeutung des Todes Jesu," in his *Der auferweckte Gekreuzigte* (Tübingen: Mohr Siebeck, 1994) 237–315 and esp. *Das Opfer*.

[7] For a more detailed description, see Jasper Hopkins, *A Companion to the Study of St. Anselm* (Minneapolis: University of Minnesota Press, 1971) esp. 187–214.

Anselm's theory of satisfaction thus employs the view of the human person as giver/doer who "ought to" perform the compensation. God remains the receiver of this satisfaction. As in the Augustinian-Thomistic grammar of sacrifice, in Anselm's theory the relational place (1) must be occupied by a human being and the place (3) by God. The analogy is not complete, since in Anselm's theory it is finally the God-man who acts at place (1).

One rather general way of reading theories of atonement is to see them as an "unbracketing" of the biblical *paradidômi* (ch. 2). The sacrifice or the atoning deed must be handed over by a human being, otherwise it does not concern humans. And the gift is to be handed over to God, not to Satan or to other humans, since otherwise it is not a sacrifice or does not compensate for the violation of God's law. In the Anselmian act of satisfaction, the God-man Jesus Christ hands himself over to God, being both the giver and the gift. In the Thomistic view of the Eucharist as sacrifice, the priest hands over Christ to God, thus performing an act of remembrance and representation which relates to Christ's self-giving act. In both acts all humans are the potential beneficiaries who can receive God's act of forgiveness and mercy as a sort of counter-gift.

Given this reading of *paradidômi* in terms of sacrifice, we may be in a position to evaluate some post-Enlightenment claims concerning the violence involved in the Christian view of satisfaction. Does this view involve a God who employs violence as a means of bringing about salvation? One, rather preliminary, apologetic strategy of answering this question might go as follows: No, since this view presupposes an anthropocentrism in which human beings bring about the allegedly violent acts of sacrifice. The view refuses to make human beings mere spectators of violent divine drama. Instead, human beings are called to carry the responsibility of their past deeds and to act themselves as agents of reconciliation.

In terms of this apology, satisfaction does not focus on punishment or violence but on reconciling the harm done. It establishes an economic logic within which human initiative is seen as a positive and necessary part of achieving forgiveness. In this sense it resembles the view of forgiveness expressed by the Lord's Prayer: human beings must themselves act mercifully in order that they can be forgiven (ch. 3). It is astonishing that whereas the human initiation of forgiveness in the Lord's Prayer has remained for centuries a major challenge for theology, the anthropocentric dimension of sacrifice has received almost no positive attention. The apology attempted here sets out to show that Anselm's anthropocentrism serves the same purpose as the human initiative of forgiveness in the Lord's Prayer.

In relation to the Lord's Prayer, theologians have felt themselves obliged to explain why and in what sense we must first forgive in order to be forgiven. In the case of sacrifice, however, modern theology has for the most part claimed that the anthropocentric view is extremely problematic and that we must not see ourselves as givers in any sacrificial sense. Modern theologians therefore claim that we must renounce all man-made sacrifices.[8] But if this is the only remaining option, we must conclude that both the Augustinian-Thomistic positive appreciation of sacrifice as a human act towards God and its Anselmian application are just dead ends. Our apologetic strategy refuses to do this.

Anselm's anthropocentrism serves the purpose of equipping human beings with the sense of responsibility. In keeping with this, the Augustinian-Thomistic grammar of sacrifice points towards a potentially nonviolent God. In *De civitate Dei* 10,6 Augustine says, modifying the biblical words (Matt 9:13), that mercy towards other humans is the true sacrifice. Since the theological meaning of sacrifice thus approaches offering and giving, there may be a positive side in the man-made sacrifice. Concerning the Lord's Prayer, we interpreted (ch. 3) interhuman forgiveness as mercy and *metanoia* which resembles but finally differs from God's forgiveness of sins. Similarly, our active mercy should initiate peacemaking and well-being among humans. It is an attitude rather than an outward action and it does not compete with God's redemptive work. Thus it resembles but finally differs from God's work. We are called to offer our mercy as an offering of reconciliation.

In sum, this would mean that (1) humans and not God are the agents of sacrifice and (2) what is required of humans is not bloodshed but mercy. If mercy is the condensate of the internal human attitude of giving and self-giving, sacrifice can perhaps be described as an ultimate externalization of actual human giving. Both mercy and sacrifice would then belong to the "scale" of positive human acts of giving. In order to become evaluated positively, however, man-made sacrifices should manifest mercy.

---

[8] Dalferth 1994 is an exemplary case of this position.

the invitation unreservedly, there would have been no Apocalypse announced and no Crucifixion."[14] This resembles the view of sacrifice as mercy in our preliminary apology above. *Metanoia* and mercy would produce the satisfaction, if any is needed.

This conclusion is a consequence of the original claim of nonviolence. Jesus proclaimed the message that we do not need sacrifices but mercy, and this message could have been accepted by "the easy way." Crucifixion manifested this message in the sense that through it, humankind comes to know, by the "indirect way," that violence is not the final answer offered in Christianity.

Girard's view of the gospel and its opposition to sacrificial violence takes very seriously the basically Augustinian and Thomistic claim that sacrifices are human attempts to relate to God. The consistently non-sacrificial account of *Things Hidden*, however, leads to a rather modernist interpretation of "the easy way." If people, after hearing Jesus' message, would have exercised *metanoia* and forgiven each other, they would have been forgiven by God. They would have realized that human attempts at sacrificial behavior would only perpetuate violence. Thus they would have become peacemakers. No atonement or sacrifice on the cross would have been necessary. This counterfactual chain of thoughts is perhaps not directly heterodox, but it is highly speculative and downplays the role of the cross in Christianity. It might be a too high price to pay for the claim that Christianity at its best would be entirely non-sacrificial.

In his more recent work, Girard has modified his view of redemption. He does not speak any more of "the easy way" in this fashion. In later works he approves of calling Jesus' death a "sacrifice" which was necessary in order that the Holy Spirit could be sent. Jesus can even be called a scapegoat "in reverse fashion, for theologically considered the initiative comes from God rather than simply from the human beings." God would thus not be violent, but he would send his Son and in so doing occupy the position (1) of the giver. Girard can also say that it is unfruitful to treat redemption as satisfaction of God's honor or justice, since the real problem lies with Satan.[15] This rather surprising and antimodernist move removes God finally from the relational place (3) of the receiver. Redemption is not achieved through the Anselmian logic

---

[14] TH 202–3.
[15] *The Girard Reader*, ed., James G. Williams (New York: Crossroad, 1996) 280; Girard, *I See Satan Fall Like Lightning* (Maryknoll, N.Y.: Orbis, 2001) 150.

of satisfaction or sacrifice, but through sending Jesus and overcoming Satan.

Without discussing Girard's elaborate theory as a whole, we may say that his struggle with the notion of sacrifice is highly instructive for our study. He completes our "preliminary apology" through creating alternatives to Anselm's theory of satisfaction. In his first attempt Girard proceeds from the idea of a completely non-sacrificial death of Jesus. This is possible but will lead into the assumption of the "easy way" which offers forgiveness without crucifixion. In a second attempt, Girard develops a more classical view within which one can speak of satisfaction without presupposing the Anselmian view of human giver and God as the receiver of satisfaction. Other theories which proceed directly from the divine initiator and take Satan into account can explain the death of Jesus. Also here one probably must pay a price. This price consists, first, of postulating Satan. Second, if the human being is not the giver and God not the receiver, there is no Anselmian economic justice, but rather a logic of free gift given by God.

Girard's creative proposals thus show us what we gain and what we lose through postulating various conceptual patterns related to sacrifice. (1) An archaic view of God who demands sacrifices is prominent in many religions. It may control but also perpetuate violence. (2) A straightforward Anselmian account makes the human being a subject of sacrificial reconciliation, but it nevertheless remains connected with the archaic view of God who operates within the economy of satisfaction. On the other hand, (3) a completely nonviolent theory of atonement would amount to the "easy way" of just consenting to Jesus' message. Even if the "easy way" after Good Friday remains counterfactual, it presents atonement in a fashion which remains predominantly cognitive: if we just learned about the hidden premises of violence, we would be saved. This is not as such modernist, but it is related to some problematic features of post-Enlightenment modernism. For these reasons, Girard finally subscribes to the non-Anselmian theory of overcoming Satan (4). This theory employs the notion of sacrifice but it is not given a decisive role.

As philosophers like Hent de Vries and Jacques Derrida[16] have remarked, the program of "sacrificing the sacrifices" necessarily remains aporetic. An enlightened person feels committed to renounce the archaic notion of sacrifice. But in renouncing this notion, the person is

[16] See de Vries 2002, 204–6.

committing nothing other than a last sacrifice. The notion thrown away for the benefit of enlightenment creeps back when this very act of renunciation is named. In this sense there is an aporia in the notion of sacrifice. This aporia is similar to, though not identical with, the already observed aporias of gift (ch. 1) and forgiveness (ch. 3). Getting rid of sacrifices is as difficult as giving a free gift. When we renounce the logic of sacrifice, we already start to employ it.

This observation matches well with the moderation that Girard has undertaken in his later elaborations. A consistent and straightforward non-sacrificial reading of the gospels leads to a sacrifice of central elements of Christianity, including the death of Jesus. It is possible to present this reading, but the price is quite high. And this price is, paradoxically, the sacrifice the interpreter has made in order to accomplish his non-sacrificial reading. A less straightforward non-sacrificial reading, attempted in Girard's later works, manages to outline an anthropology in which "the easy way" does not play a role and in which the passion story is prominent. This reading ascribes to God some role in "orchestrating" the salvation event that may contain some violent and sacrificial aspects. At the same time, it seeks to avoid the problems of the Anselmian logic of economy and satisfaction through replacing them with theocentric giving and the gift.

In sum, we have observed that there are various apologetic strategies to relieve the tension between sacrifice on the one hand and the need of nonviolence on the other. (a) One can say that sacrifice in Augustinian-Thomistic vocabulary is not a divine but a human act. In addition, (b) one can interpret the human act as an act of mercy rather than an external sacrifice. In order to account for the claim that God nevertheless demands or orchestrates the violent death of Jesus, (c) one can develop the Augustinian view as René Girard does in *Things Hidden* by claiming that God does not demand any kind of sacrificial behavior but only mercy. Thus the death of Jesus would not be a sacrifice.

If this sounds too liberal or modernistic, one can finally moderate the non-sacrificial reading in various ways. We may say that the Anselmian-Thomistic grammar should be modified (d) by speaking of God not as the receiver of satisfaction but as the giver of salvation. Instead of approving Anselm's view of satisfaction we could (e) understand redemption as overcoming Satan's power. Given (d) and (e), we can speak (f) of Christ as sacrifice or as a scapegoat who is sent not in order to appease God but in order to lay bare the secret of violence, to overcome evil and to show us the grace of God. None of the alternatives (d to f) provide as such a sufficient explanation of the death of Jesus, but they all alleviate the tensions and opt for a modified nonviolence in the theology of redemption.

The Eucharistic Sacrifice: Luther's Contribution

We saw how René Girard views the sacrifice of a scapegoat in a "reverse fashion" so that God through sending Jesus occupies the place (1) of the giver. This view goes against the Anselmian theology of satisfaction. Girard replaces this view with a more theocentric perspective in which God's act of offering or sending Jesus can only be called sacrifice in a secondary sense. This perspective of theocentric giving has a certain parallel in the extensive Reformation discussions around sacrifice. They concern the role of the eucharistic sacrifice and its relationship to the death of Christ.

For Martin Luther and his colleague Philip Melanchthon, the eucharistic sacrifice performed in the medieval Mass had too close a connection with the satisfaction made in the death of Christ. The Reformers claimed that the Mass was misused to grant forgiveness not only to the participants but even to absent and dead people who were counted among the beneficiaries of this sacrifice. The benefit obtained through performing the eucharistic sacrifice was employed in a way that made forgiveness a business in which you can buy Masses offered for the sake of some dead or absent beneficiary. Thus the Augustinian-Thomistic grammar of sacrifice becomes misused so that a priest who celebrates the Mass privately can nevertheless obtain forgiveness for absent beneficiaries.[17]

We will not discuss here in detail whether this criticism was justified. At least concerning the position of Thomas Aquinas described above, it was an exaggeration, since Thomas does not outline a theory of automatic benefits. On the contrary, he makes the power of satisfaction dependent on the subjective devotion of the priest and the beneficiaries. Thus we cannot deduce from Thomas a mechanical production of forgiveness through the mere performance of the eucharistic sacrifice. On the other hand, Thomas does say that in a secondary or "concomitant" manner the eucharistic sacrifice "has the power of rendering satisfaction" (Sth III q79 a5). Although this power is dependent both

---

[17] In addition to Simon 2003, Frank C. Senn, *Christian Liturgy: Catholic and Evangelical* (Minneapolis: Fortress, 1997) 240–356, gives a good historical picture.

on the believer's union with Christ and on the fervor of his or her devotion, it is true that the eucharistic sacrifice can be interpreted in such
a way that it is able to produce forgiveness.

Our discussion of Reformation criticism concerns more its systematic development of the understanding of sacrifice than its historical
accuracy. The Lutheran reformers very consciously emphasized the
ephapax, the view that Jesus Christ brought the satisfaction for all sins
"once and for all," as the *Augsburg Confession* states. In its understanding of crucifixion, the Lutheran Confessions remain rather Anselmian.
But concerning the Lord's Supper, its consistent emphasis on *ephapax*
does not leave much theological role to the eucharistic sacrifice. This
sacrifice "does not merit the forgiveness of sins or reconciliation but is
rendered by those who have already been reconciled as a way for us to
give thanks or express gratitude for having received forgiveness."[18]

This view is not so far from Thomas Aquinas as it seems to be.
Like Thomas, the Lutheran Confessions make a distinction between
sacrament and sacrifice. Interestingly, it employs the relational places
of giving as a criterion for this distinction: "A sacrament is a ceremony
or work in which God gives to us what the promise joined to the ceremony offers. . . . By contrast, a sacrifice is a ceremony or work that
we render to God in order to give him honor."[19] This definition comes
rather close to Thomas's distinction in Sth III q79 a5, although the
point of sacramental giving is made more strongly by the Lutheran
Reformers.

Given both the traditional definition of sacrifice as human offering
to God and the fundamental sufficiency of the *ephapax*, the Lutheran
Confessions claim that the eucharistic sacrifice can only be understood
as thanksgiving and gratitude. God is giving the sacrament, the community of believers receives it. If we put humans in the relational place
(1) of the giver, they can at this place give thanks or express gratitude,
but they cannot produce anything sacrificial. Even the *eucharistikon*,
that is, this sacrifice of thanksgiving, is not an act of giving that initi-
ates or produces anything new. It is rather a response or a counter-gift
which reflects the initial position of the human being as a receiver.

This does not mean, however, that the element of human offering
becomes minimized in Lutheran worship. After the power of human

---

[18] Augsburg Confession 24; Apology 24, in *The Book of Concord* (= BC), eds., Robert
Kolb and Timothy Wengert (Minneapolis: Fortress, 2000) 71 and 261.

[19] BC 260f.

offerings to make satisfaction is denied, the view of the human being as a responsive giver comprehends almost everything in Christian worship and life: "Now the rest are eucharistic sacrifices, which are called 'sacrifices of praise', namely, the preaching of the gospel, faith, prayer, thanksgiving, confession, . . . They are performed by those who are already reconciled."[20]

We observed in chapter 3 how Lutheran theology understands God as giver and humans as receivers. This basic structure is also characteristic of a Lutheran theology of the Eucharist. In its sacramental dimension, God gives the Eucharist to the believer. God forgives and reconciles. When human being is put into the place (1) of the giver in relation to God, human behavior can only be responsive: we are giving thanks and expressing our gratitude for the good already received.

Because of this basic structure, Lutheranism and most other branches of Protestantism are critical of the Roman Catholic idea that the priest performs a sacrifice to God at the altar. This idea is incompatible with the basic structure of giving and receiving. At the same time it should be emphasized that Lutherans and other Protestants have often only received a caricature of Roman Catholic eucharistic teaching. The *Augsburg Confession*, for instance, outlines the refuted view as follows: "Jesus Christ had made satisfaction by his death only for original sin and had instituted the Mass as a sacrifice for other sins. Thus, the Mass was made into a sacrifice for the living and the dead for the purpose of taking away sin and appeasing God."[21] The anthropocentric element contained in the traditional notion of sacrifice is here exaggerated and made into a forgiveness automatically obtained by the priest.

In the ecumenical movement of the twentieth century, these exaggerations have become moderated and the underlying structures discovered. This does not mean, however, that all differences have become insignificant. There seems to be an underlying confessional difference between the anthropocentric tradition of Catholicism and the theocentric theology of the Lutheran Reformation. Lutherans clearly emphasize God as giver and, consequently, stress the sacramental nature of the Eucharist and downplay its sacrificial meaning. Catholics share the basic sacramental view, within which the human being is spoken of as receiver, as Thomas Aquinas says in Sth III q79 a5.

[20] BC 262.
[21] Augsburg Confession 24, in BC 68–70.

But Catholics have also preserved the sacrificial meaning in which the priest not only gives thanks but offers the sacrificial gift to God. Thus the *Catechism of the Catholic Church* repeats the statement from the Council of Trent that at the Last Supper Jesus Christ left to the church a visible sacrifice by which the salutary power of the sacrifice of the cross would "be applied to the forgiveness of the sins we daily commit."[22] Since it is the priest who performs this visible sacrifice, we can still today speak of Catholic anthropocentrism, that is, of the active role of the human being who brings about the sacrifice and in so doing gives something sacred to God.

It is very difficult to say whether there is a qualitative or only a quantitative theological difference between Catholic anthropocentrism and Protestant theocentrism in this respect. Protestants can speak of a sacrifice of praise and thanksgiving, a responsive sacrifice, or a counter-gift. Catholics can on their part say that the priest is not initiating anything new, but is re-presenting and re-membering a past event.[23] Thus the Catholic sacrifice can also be understood as a response. Nevertheless, the Catholic priest is an agent or a giver in a much stronger sense than his Protestant colleague.

Lutheran criticism of sacrifices in a way resembles René Girard's attempt at a non-sacrificial reading of Christianity. In both, sacrifices appear as problematic: they are violent and express an anthropocentric view of reality in which the human being exercises control over the sacred. Moreover, René Girard's first interpretation ("the easy way") of redemption resembles some liberal forms of Protestant theology: redemption is cognitive enlightenment, blood is not really necessary. Somewhat paradoxically, Girard's second interpretation, redemption as overcoming Satan, resembles Martin Luther's own view in which the battle with Satan and even the patristic topic of "cheating Satan" receive significant attention.[24]

On closer inspection, however, there is a difference. The Lutheran Confessions find the Anselmian theory of satisfaction rather unproblematic; their criticism is related to the eucharistic sacrifice. In Girard, the real target is Anselm's view of satisfaction. The observation of this difference may also point to some internal problems of Lutheran

[22] *Catechism of the Catholic Church* (London: Chapman, 1994) 1366.
[23] *Catechism*, 1356–81.
[24] See in more detail Risto Saarinen, "René Girard and Lutheran Theology," in *Theophilos 1*, 2001, 317–38, and Heiko A. Oberman, *Luther, der Mensch zwischen Gott und Teufel* (Berlin: Severin und Siedler, 1981).

theology. An extreme concentration on the "once and for all" nature of crucifixion and a complete denial of human agency in performing sacrifice may make the problem of divine violence even more virulent. Catholic theology may be able to moderate this problem to some extent through pointing to the anthropocentric nature of sacrifice. God may orchestrate human history, but it is nevertheless a human history in which God maintains some distance from violence. Given this, we may still blame Anselm's God for pedantry and for the "orchestration" of violence, since forgiveness is not freely granted but a human satisfaction is demanded.

In Lutheranism, God seems to be more directly involved with both good and evil. God is considered as a giver of everything, even the sacrificial death of Christ—we saw in chapter 2 that Luther's *Large Catechism* says that in Christ "God . . . has given himself."[25] But the view of an overall theocentric giving evokes the problem of evil and violence: are they directly given by God as well? One way to conceptualize this dynamic is to call it, as we did with Girard, a "price" of purchasing an explanation. Lutherans want to get rid of anthropocentric interpretations of the eucharistic sacrifice. In order to do this, they apply the basic idea of God as giver and the human being as receiver. As a result of this application, humans can only act sacrificially in terms of responsive thanksgiving and praise. This may be an elegant theocentric explanation of eucharistic theology, but it has little bearing on the problem of divine violence. It may even make matters worse, since the theocentric giving of "everything" makes God directly responsible for evil and violence as well.

Among other things, this remark serves the purpose of saying that "anthropocentric" is not necessarily a pejorative word. When human beings act as givers, they are responsible persons and not just innocent bystanders. When Thomas claims that the devotion of the offerer and the congregation can, through the union with Christ, even transmit Christ's forgiving power, the human being is taken into the communion and not left to remain a spectator. For these reasons, it is not quite evident that "automatism" goes together with the sacrificial interpretation of the Eucharist in the way the Reformers thought. One may even make a counter-claim and say that the theocentric view as such rather promotes automatism than prevents it.

---

[25] BC 434.

When the Lutheran Reformers criticize automatism and claim that personal faith is required in the reception of the Eucharist, they also recommend personal involvement. In this involvement, the human person does not appear as giver or a doer, but he or she is nevertheless involved. Faith's response is a personal act. In this sense, the human element is there in both the Catholic and Lutheran traditions, either as an active devotion or as a faithful reception. Given this, the Lutheran criticism of Roman Catholic devotional life seems to be exaggerated or based on accidental abuses. On closer examination, both sides appreciate personal involvement and reject automatism.

The Lutheran view is in fact richer than the above quotations from *The Book of Concord* make it seem. It is not limited to exaggerated accusations, but has a positive side as well. The basic proclamation of Lutheranism has been that God does not want our sacrifices, because everything is already reconciled. Thus in the Eucharist we can concentrate on the sacrament of the real presence of Christ and its spiritual nourishment. We need not consider the sacrificial aspect. This has been emphasized in Lutheran eucharistic liturgies which have avoided the concept of sacrifice. Understood in this fashion, there is a nonviolent God who is the giver of everything and does not count our deeds with a logic of exchange. The paradigm of free gift is primary, and within this paradigm reconciliation is not seen in terms of *facere debet homo*, that is, of human merits. The absence of this anthropocentrism may be a non-Anselmian and a potentially nonviolent feature of Lutheranism.

This emphasis might come more directly from Martin Luther than from *The Book of Concord* which, as we have seen, keeps the traditional understanding of sacrifice as a human act and presupposes Anselm's theory of satisfaction. Luther can employ the traditional four-place relation creatively in order to outline a new understanding of sacrifice. He is not just emphasizing the *ephapax* and abandoning the view of the Eucharist as sacrifice. Instead, he can claim that the Eucharist, in addition to human praise and thanksgiving, does contain a peculiar type of Christ-centered sacrifice, as Wolfgang Simon[26] points out.

This surprising finding for many Lutherans goes as follows: human beings can offer something to God, namely, themselves. This self-giving is a spiritual sacrifice. It does not mean martyrdom, but one's becoming a loving servant of one's neighbors. Of course, this is not an offering that makes satisfaction, but a faithful response to the

[26] Simon 2003, 373–89.

preceding act of God and thus in some sense parallel to thanksgiving. At the same time, this spiritual offering can be understood as an act in which Christ occupies the position (1) of the giver. Christ gives the believers as a gift to the Father so that humankind may benefit from this giving. The spiritual service of neighborly love is fundamentally initiated by Christ, who presents this service as a gift to the Father. This is also a spiritual meaning of eucharistic sacrifice. As the real host at the altar, Christ offers the faithful to the Father in order that they may serve one another and act for each other's sake. In this first identification, humans thus become both the spiritual gift (2) and the beneficiaries (4).[27]

The spiritual meaning is connected with Luther's view that it is Christ, not the priest, who presides at the altar. In the Eucharist, Christ is both the giver (1) and the gift (2). As in the passion story and in the biblical *paradidômi*, it is Christ's self-giving which is the sacrifice at the altar. Not the priest, but Christ is the giver. This second identification of the giver with the gift makes it possible to say that in spite of the new understanding of the priest's role, there is nevertheless a connection between *ephapax* and the altar, since in both Christ gives himself. This understanding was not totally Luther's innovation, for the idea of Christ as the primary giver (*principalis offerens*) can be found in earlier sources. But Luther gives it a new relative importance.[28]

Whereas the second identification is biblical, the first identification between the gift (2) and the beneficiaries (4) is more complex. Within the traditional grammar of sacrifice, it was difficult to identify the gift with the beneficiaries, since the underlying economic exchange presupposes that the beneficiaries are debtors whose debt is covered by the gift. When the faithful in the spiritual sacrifice become both the gift and the beneficiaries, the economic logic is surpassed. In Christian love I give myself for your sake, and you give yourself for my sake. Thus we are both gifts and beneficiaries of this mutual service which is initiated by Christ. This breaks the traditional logic of sacrifice rather dramatically.[29]

In this spiritual human self-giving it is the "poietic account" of the Golden Rule which serves as a horizon of understanding. As we saw in chapter 2, Luther understands the rule of neighborly love (Matt 7:12; Luke 6:31) in terms of fulfilling your neighbor's lacks and needs. This

---

[27] Simon 2003, 294–98, 373–80. Cf. e.g. WA 6, 368–69; WA 8, 415–23 and 486–95; Augustine, *De civitate Dei* 10, 4–6.
[28] Simon 2003, 298–300.
[29] Simon 2003, 373–79.

poietic filling and covering for the needs of others is not an autonomous activity, but a response to and imitation of divine agape: Christ gave himself for our sake, he gave the gift we needed. In a parallel manner we are called to give ourselves to the service of our neighbors, filling their needs and giving them gifts, as we also need, expect, and receive gifts. This "spiritual sacrifice" is not a work of mediation, but it is a response or a reflex of the model given by Christ. Christ gave himself as gift, but in addition to this gift he also gave a model of Christian love. This love has a form of self-giving. Its character is "a posteriori," after the salvific event of Jesus Christ.[30]

Thus Luther's elaboration of "spiritual sacrifice" goes deeper than the relatively traditional formulations of *The Book of Concord*. Luther boldly reorganizes and to an extent merges the different placeholders of the Augustinian-Thomist grammar of sacrifice. By so doing he is able to point out not only the theocentric, but basically christocentric character of the eucharistic sacrifice. On the one hand this move supports the idea of the Lutheran Confessions that the priest does not perform the sacrifice. On the other hand, however, it allows for a quasi-sacrificial interpretation of the Eucharist. This reinterpretation is primarily christological: the figure of Christ's self-giving (places 1 and 2) creates a connection between the cross and the altar without compromising the *ephapax*. Secondarily, the reinterpretation is anthropological in the sense that the human person reappears as giver of the "spiritual" sacrifice. Within this mode, human beings give themselves and thus become both the gift and the beneficiary (places 2 and 4). Humans are thus called to serve one another in self-giving. The primary and secondary modes reflect the "poietic account" of divine agape in which the first, christocentric self-giving is salvific, whereas the second, interhuman self-giving, through reflecting the first one, enables love among humans.

As in Girard, we notice in Martin Luther and in Lutheranism two successive moves: there is a first move of renouncing all sacrifices, and a second counter-move of reinterpreting the sacrifices. The second move does not, however, compromise the first. It is rather a move embedded in the very logic of sacrifice. As we have observed, it is more or less impossible to "sacrifice the sacrifices," since this very act already contains a sacrifice. The second move is therefore necessary, but it does not falsify the first move. In speaking of sacrifice, it is necessary both to

---

[30] Simon 2003, 374.

be critical of sacrifice and to aim at reinterpreting or moderating it. The first move is connected with many reasons: we must renounce the view that we can control everything by our own acts, we are called to be critical of religious violence that often takes the form of sacrifice, we need to see beyond the logic of satisfaction and compensation that is embedded in the economy of sacrifice.

The second move also brings some positive element of "anthropocentrism" into the otherwise theocentric Lutheran view of sacrifice. Within the realm of spiritual sacrifice, the human being is seen as an agent and as a giver. This is the personal involvement of a Christian. Although Christ accomplishes everything, we are not mere spectators. The model of Christ's self-giving is transferred to us as a spiritual sacrifice, a responsive behavior within which we become agents and givers of praise and thanksgiving, but also givers of concrete service for the sake of our neighbor. Because the second move moderates the theocentric basic attitude, we can perhaps say that Lutherans are not so far from Catholic eucharistic theology as their harsh criticism seems to indicate on first hearing.

Thanksgiving and Liturgy

One important ecumenical area of controversy is the theology of liturgy. Traditional controversies originated around the notion of sacrifice, and the different views of sacrifice found their expression in different eucharistic liturgies. Churches that are today in the process of renewing their worship life face again the old controversies. A more profound account of the theology of giving and especially of thanksgiving may be helpful in discussing liturgical renewal. Therefore we will devote some attention to thanksgiving and to the eucharistic liturgy as the last section of this chapter. Liturgy is a concrete example of how the theology of giving works in practice.

Because Lutheranism wanted to see God as giver and replaced human sacrifices with Christ's self-giving, the earliest Lutheran liturgies did not employ the traditional Roman Eucharistic Prayer. Luther removed almost the entire Eucharistic Prayer from the liturgy, because he considered its sacrificial terminology to be profoundly mistaken. In addition, he believed that most of the Roman canon was a medieval invention, created to suit the underlying doctrine of eucharistic sacrifice. Thus the canon of the Mass did not reflect early Christianity.

Historically, Luther was wrong. The Eucharistic Prayer and essential parts of the Roman canon are much older than their sacrificial reading against which Luther was fighting. Luther's undifferentiated amputation of the Eucharistic Prayer from the liturgy has therefore been regarded as a profoundly wrong decision by many later liturgists. Advocates of liturgical renewal and ecumenically minded scholars of the early church have argued that Lutherans and other Protestants should again include the Eucharistic Prayer in their liturgies. This has happened in many churches. As a result, contemporary Protestant worship life has begun to resemble more the liturgies of Roman Catholic and Orthodox churches.[31]

Many liturgists have presented their historical diagnosis as follows: the medieval Latin church developed in a problematic direction because it adopted the doctrine of transsubstantiation and emphasized the sacrificial dimension of the Eucharist. The liturgical tradition of the early church was, however, centered around the Eucharist, understood literally as *eucharistein*, as thanksgiving, praise, and recollection. At the Communion table, salvation history was remembered and reenacted through liturgy. Early eucharistic prayers stress this dimension of memory and employ praise and thanksgiving as a response to the salvific act of Christ. This dimension of the early church was to an extent lost in medieval Latin liturgy.

Luther's reform did not provide any real help. On the contrary, it made the matters worse by deleting the Eucharistic Prayer. When the eucharistic liturgy was reduced more or less to the words of institution, the dogmatic and theoretical issue of real presence became dominant, while the eucharistic dimension, the responsive and communal perspective of remembering and thanksgiving, was lost. In this sense Luther, in spite of his vehement criticism of medieval abuses, continued along the wrong path. In addition, Luther's false picture of the history of the liturgy motivated his fatal decision to amputate the Eucharistic Prayer.

This diagnosis[32] has recently been challenged by Dorothea Wendebourg. It is instructive to look at her counter-diagnosis more closely. In

---

[31] See Senn 1997 and R.C.D. Jasper and C. J. Cuming, *Prayers of the Eucharist: Early and Reformed*, 3rd ed. (Collegeville: Liturgical Press, 1992).

[32] This is basically Dorothea Wendebourg's description in: "Den falschen Weg Roms zu Ende gegangen?" in her *Die eine Christenheit auf Erden* (Tübingen: Mohr Siebeck, 2000) 164–94, here: 164–68, as well as in "Noch einmal: Den falschen Weg Roms zu Ende gegangen?" in *Zeitschrift für Theologie und Kirche 99*, 2002, 400–40. Among others, she is criticizing Gregory Dix, *The Shape of the Liturgy* (New York: Seabury Press, 1982). Cf. also Senn 1997, 274–85, 476–79, 651–57.

following her argument, it is important to note that we are not only concerned with a historical debate, but with the theologically adequate shape of contemporary Christian worship. Wendebourg sets out to defend Luther's reforms and the subsequent Protestant developments. In addition, she is critical of some recent ecumenical attempts to bring back the eucharistic tradition of the early church into the liturgies of contemporary denominations.

The liturgists have supported their diagnosis with the historical finding that the words of institution appear at a relatively late stage in the development of the eucharistic liturgy. Declaring them to be the only decisive part of the Eucharistic Prayer, as Luther did, must therefore be a false decision. Until the fourth century, significant parts of Christianity could celebrate the Eucharist without mentioning the words of institution. Wendebourg does not question this history, but she defends the Protestant view with an argument that at first appears as traditionalist Roman Catholic. The words of institution, she claims, may be historically younger than some other liturgical phrases, but they are nevertheless theologically primary. The historical development shows that they must obtain a central place in the eucharistic liturgy. They are biblical and thus bring the tradition of the Synoptic Gospels and of the apostle Paul into the liturgy.[33]

When Luther set aside other parts of the Eucharistic Prayer, he did not commit any theological mistake. His theological judgment was right: the words of institution are central, irrespective of the exact date of their appearance in the liturgy. He might have erred concerning the historical sequence of the liturgical developments, but he weighed the theological outcome rightly. This can be seen if we examine the element of thanksgiving. Giving thanks and praise is important throughout worship, not only in the Eucharist. Thus, mere thanksgiving does not identify the Eucharist. Moreover, thanks and praise cannot initiate anything, since they are by definition human responses. In addition to them, a primary gift is needed. Seeing the Eucharist in terms of mere thanksgiving would thus be insufficient and even misleading. The words of institution are, and here Luther is right, creative acts in which Christ appears as giver, is giving himself.[34]

The words of institution are the theologically primary elements of the Eucharist. They initiate, they offer the gift, and as consecratory

---

[33] Wendebourg 2000, 170–71.
[34] Wendebourg 2000, 192–93.

words even become the means of grace. Human thanksgiving and praise cannot do those things, however ancient they are in liturgical texts. Because the words of institution make God the giver and "institute" the reality at hand, they are primary.[35] This was also the insight which made them central from the fourth century onwards. When Luther liberated the words of institution from the sacrificial phraseology of the Roman canon, he did not continue along a false path, but set the theological perspective right.

Wendebourg's provocative defense of Luther's renewal has prompted a lively debate in Germany, especially since her argument seems to question many liturgical changes which employ the ecumenical material available in the *Baptism, Eucharist and Ministry* (BEM) document of the World Council of Churches. BEM recommends a rich eucharistic liturgy which takes seriously the concentration on thanksgiving in the early liturgies. At the same time, BEM ascribes a central place to the words of institution and considers the Eucharist to be "essentially the sacrament of the gift."[36]

Wendebourg considers, however, that BEM is at variance with the Lutheran view, since in emphasizing thanksgiving BEM loses the fundamental view of the Lord's Supper as "a divine gift which the congregation receives." She argues that in order to preserve the "dialogical character" of the liturgy, as demanded by both herself and her critics, one must put the words of institution at the center, as Luther did. They are God's word, they give the gift. The elements of thanksgiving are a response, and thus a dialogue emerges. If the eucharistic elements of thanksgiving dominate the liturgy, this dialogue is lost and the Lord's Supper becomes "a unilateral action in which the congregation does not receive, but turns to God in thanking, praying, and offering."[37]

In other words, Wendebourg's theological concern is to preserve the theology of the gift. This is only possible if God is seen as giver and the congregation as a receiver. Wendebourg's aim is not to defend liturgical reductionism: she emphasizes dialogue and considers thanksgiving to be a proper liturgical response. Her point is that thanksgiving is by definition secondary, whereas the gift is and should be primary.

---

[35] Wendebourg 2000, 190.

[36] "Baptism, Eucharist and Ministry" in *Growth in Agreement, Reports and Agreed Statements of Ecumenical Conversations on a World Level*, ed., Harding Meyer et al. (Geneva: World Council of Churches, 1984) 465–503, here: Eucharist 2, Ministry 13.

[37] Wendebourg 2002, 413 and 404.

Here we see the Lutheran view of God as giver and the Lord's Supper as a theocentric event.

There are many ways to relate to Wendebourg's criticism. One can say that her view is nevertheless compatible with BEM, since this document does emphasize the gift and the words of institution. One can even grant her view that a historically later development is theologically primary, and still claim that early eucharistic prayers without the words of institution can be regarded as valid. Their validity does not come from their age, but rather follows from Wendebourg's own claim: since the eucharistic thanksgiving is understood as response, there simply must be the preceding primary gift. This is the case even when Jesus's words of institution are not explicitly recited in the Eucharistic Prayer, for the very act of thanksgiving witnesses to the gift. Thus one may claim that the earliest liturgies nevertheless presuppose the preceding gift and that their thanksgiving is by no means a unilateral human action towards God.

We will not, however, enter the historical or confessional debate at this point. Instead, we can briefly ask whether our project of outlining a theology of giving and the gift has anything to contribute to this debate. Wendebourg does not refine her concept of the gift, but her commitment to the view that the gift goes together with a dialogical character of the worship already shows something. It is symptomatic of a reciprocity surrounding the gift.

In some settings of Lutheran theology, e.g., in the theology of baptism (Introduction) and especially in the theology of justification (Introduction and ch. 3), the gift is often interpreted as a unilateral event. God is the giver and we are receivers who are not supposed to enter into a dialogue concerning salvation. As we have seen, however, even monergistic Lutherans do presuppose some kind of openness or responsivity with regard to the reception of salvation. When Wendebourg insists that a consistent emphasis on the primacy of the gift strengthens the dialogue, understood as response, she also connects salvific monergism with the openness and responsivity of the receivers.

Therefore, her theological point that the words of institution must be given primary importance in order that thanksgiving makes sense and a responsive dialogue can emerge, is basically correct. Saying this does not imply anything with regard to whether the eucharistic dialogue should be conceptualized in the same manner as the theology of justification and baptism. Conceding her theological point only affirms that such a dialogical character is central to the Eucharist.

Even if this point is conceded, it is nevertheless a different question whether other approaches to the theology of the Eucharist are as problematic as Wendebourg claims them to be. There is at least one contradiction in Wendebourg's own argument, since she first says that thanksgiving cannot initiate the presence of Christ but only acts as a response to it and then claims that liturgists who emphasize thanksgiving and praise make the eucharistic liturgy a unilateral human action towards God.[38] If all parties subscribe to the first statement, as I think they should, then no one would subscribe to the second. This in turn means that even those liturgists who stress the eucharistic character of the liturgy in fact do preserve its dialogical character.

In addition to this conceptual or qualitative argument, one can employ a quantitative argument which concerns the relative amount of theocentric gift and anthropocentric thanksgiving in the eucharistic interplay. In other words: if the Eucharistic Prayer centers around our recollection and our thanksgiving, does this diminish the relative importance and primacy of the gift? I think that in the light of the philosophical discussion undertaken in chapter 1, the answer is: no. Consequently, Wendebourg's point that an emphasis on thanksgiving downplays the gift[39] does not hold.

Let us look at this quantitative argument more closely. If a gift is given so that the receiver does not even realize that it is a gift, we are in doubt what this act is. Is the agent just "putting" something somewhere, as we said in the introduction? Both anthropologists and philosophers think that a gift brings about an awareness and also a feeling of gratitude, even indebtedness in the receiver. In Pierre Bourdieu's theory (ch. 1), the gift is only defined through the counter-act which emerges as result of giving something. Of course, this does not fully match with the theological theories of the gift. But at the level of common sense, the gift needs to be comprehended as a gift. In this very comprehension, a feeling of gratitude and indebtedness emerges. Thus gratitude indicates the gift rather than downplays it.

Derrida's wrestling with the gift (ch. 1) bears an interesting analogy to Wendebourg's criticism. On the one hand, the primacy of free giving and the gift must be preserved, since otherwise there is no gift. At the same time, however, this freedom is immediately contaminated through the response of the receivers. But this response is necessary in

---

[38] Wendebourg 2000, 193 and 2002, 404.
[39] Wendebourg 2002, 404–18.

order that we can speak of a gift in the first place. Thus we move in a circle or within an aporia: we must define a gift both from the perspective of the giver and from the perspective of the receiver. But these perspectives do not meet or they even exclude each other. Wendebourg sees the second exclusion through which the act of thanksgiving spoils the gift. But she neglects the first exclusion through which the gift destroys itself through its denial of a grateful reception.

In this aporia, Marion's project of "bracketing" both the giver and the receiver (ch. 1) represents a middle perspective. The gift shines amidst the phenomenological reality we conceptualize as givenness. In this givenness it is we who, in an encounter with this reality, perform the conceptualization. Thus phenomenology is a responsive undertaking. In terms of this phenomenological analysis, we may reformulate our quantitative argument as follows, reducing the historical details to a minimum: early Christianity conceptualized the eucharistic liturgy in terms of recollection and thanksgiving. In so doing, they reenacted the salvation event and saw the Eucharist in terms of the givenness of this event and in terms of the gift present at the Eucharist. The conceptualization of this givenness was necessarily a responsive undertaking: recollecting, reenacting, and giving thanks.

Of course, this response did not initiate the gift. The gift was there in the givenness; the original giver was both absent and present. The richness of the liturgical response did not downplay the gift, but rather showed its richness and primacy. The responsive human reenactment was thus no competitor of the gift, but highlighted it. In the long run, it was probably necessary and proper to name the gift: the words of institution were added and gave a name to the gift itself. Thus the gift became central also in the text of the Eucharistic Prayer, but it was central as the givenness of the liturgical situation from the beginning. Seen in this way, the quantitative argument simply says that the richness of thanksgiving rather supports the gift than downplays it.

In this sense both Wendebourg and the liturgists have a point. Luther did not proceed on a false path, but corrected the exaggerated anthropocentrism of the sacrificial Roman canon. But neither did the integration of the words of institution initiate any problematic development, since these words named the event which was there from the beginning. We may even say, as Wendebourg[40] does, that the Western understanding of these words as words of consecration was not funda-

---

[40] Wendebourg 2000, 180.

mentally problematic, since this development only brought about the necessary differentiation between divine and human action within the drama of salvation. The original giver may only have been present within the givenness of the reenactment, but from a certain historical stage onwards the giver is named and an adequate differentiation takes place.

Finally, we draw attention to one text of Luther that has been neglected by liturgists. In his late lectures on Genesis, Luther describes the Sabbath service of Adam and his descendants in paradise. In this ideal form of worship which was not contaminated by human works of self-righteousness, the liturgy consisted for the most part of praise and thanksgiving. At the same time, this praise was not a monologue of humans: it was a response to the greatest gift (*summum beneficium*), the creation of humans according to the likeness of God.[41] In this sense the first and ideal worship preserved the gift of God, although it at the same time was structured according to *eucharistein*, praise and thanksgiving.

[41] WA 42, 80, 20–81, 4. LW 1, 103–5.

5

Giving an Example—Being Gifted

In previous chapters we have observed various instances of a phenomenon in which the particular form of giving at hand is accompanied with "giving an example" or "giving a model." A child who receives a Christmas present also receives an understanding of what it is to give. In addition to the gift, the child receives a model, and in learning this model the child hopefully also learns to give (ch. 1). When Christ gives himself and loves humans with his poietic agape, human beings receive not only this love, but also a "rule of divine love," a model of purposive action which does not only desire the inherent values of its object, but is able to give to the needy. In learning this rule, human beings are called to love their neighbors in a similar way, covering their needs and lacks. Thus, agape is accompanied with a calling or a task (ch. 2)

Concerning forgiveness, the example of mercy has a similar, though not identical, effect. A merciful person gives a model, and this model is extremely important in the creation of such interhuman attitudes which reflect the culture of peace and tolerance rather than of violence and punitive justice. Interhuman forgiveness is so important because it shapes the spirit of the whole community (ch. 3). Even the ambivalent topic of sacrifice gave Luther, after all criticism of human sacrifices, a possibility to speak of "spiritual sacrifice" in which humans serve each other with mercy and poietic love of neighbor. In this interhuman spiritual sacrifice, Christ's self-giving for the sake of humanity is reflected in diaconal terms: We give ourselves to the service of God, not to offer something to God, but in order that our neighbors can benefit from this service. In this sense, the sacrificial love of Jesus Christ gives us an example (ch. 4).

In sum, various forms of giving are accompanied with a mimetic and contagious effect. They give a model which is followed by others. Learning through imitation or modeling is a basic phenomenon among living beings, both humans and non-humans. It is of course not limited to acts of giving, but is typical for many kinds of behavior. For several reasons it is instructive to have a closer look at this phenomenon of giving an example or a model. First, we have here a case that need not be one of intentional giving. One can give a good or a bad example without intending it. At the same time, it is proper to call imitation a sort of giving, since imitation and learning through models presuppose a living giver, a gift (often a pattern of behavior) which becomes transmitted, and a living receiver. As we saw in the introduction, this three-place relation and the qualification of giver and receiver as animated typically characterize giving and receiving.

Giving a model is, however, a rather untypical or even metaphorical way of giving. The gift is transmitted, but the giver does not lose anything. In the contagious act of imitation, a behavioral pattern is spread in a way which seems to increase the quantity of the gift in each step of transmission. Giving an example is like a horn of plenty: as a giver you can duplicate and propagate the gift without limits and yet keep it at your disposal. In addition, this may be intentional or nonintentional. We are therefore dealing with an extremely complex subspecies of giving.

A second reason for the importance of this topic lies in its rich history in Christian tradition. Imitation has always been of paramount importance in religious formation and spiritual aspiration. The idea of distributing something without losing it is central for the theology of evangelization and proclamation. Still another dimension of "giving an example" can be found in the theology of the icon and religious painting. Icons are models which give an example of Christian life. They are both formative and spiritual, and they do not lose any of their quantity or quality in transmitting their message of the Christian model.

Third, the topics of mimesis and imitation are also central to philosophy, the history of education, and the history of art. We cannot deal with all these dimensions of culture, but it is important to realize that theological imitation has its counterparts in various other forms of human culture.

In order to create a perspective from which this vast field of giving a model can be approached, we will briefly outline René Girard's theory of mimetic desire. Even if we would not finally adopt Girard's elaborate cultural anthropology, it is a platform from which various topics can be fruitfully observed.

Mimesis and Disengagement

We live amidst of a rich plurality of models and patterns of behavior. If somebody asks us why we follow some examples instead of others, we might answer that these particular models catch our attention and interest. We desire some things, but not everything. Our choosing a particular model would thus be dependent on our fundamental desires. Given this, the next question concerns the desires. Where do they come from? Are they an innate part of our nature, or has somebody manipulated us to desire particular objects and patterns of behavior? To this we may answer that some desires, like the desire for food and drink, sexual desire, and perhaps also the general desire for personal recognition, are probably innate. But more particular and contingent desires, for instance a preference for a particular kind of food, for a special type of clothing, an appreciation of some professions above others, and so on, we have probably learned. Our social environment has conditioned us to desire them.

René Girard's view of mimetic desire focuses on this last point. He claims that most of our desires are learned through an imitation of some model. The model is not chosen on the basis of the need created by the already active desire. The causality follows a reverse order: it is the model that activates and establishes the desire. Human beings have a tendency to attach themselves to models; what we call desire often simply means that this attachment to some model has been established. Thus we learn to desire things through mimesis. We learn to imitate the desires of others. Human desire is not caused by its object but it is born from the observation that my companions already desire this object. Imitation is thus not limited to external behavior, but even our emotions and desires are a product of mimesis.[1]

In this way Girard radicalizes both the concept of mimesis and the phenomenology of desires and emotions. We need not discuss here

---

[1] René Girard, *Violence and the Sacred* (= VS; Baltimore: Johns Hopkins Press, 1977) 145–49.

whether even the most basic desires, such as hunger and sexual desire, follow this pattern of modeling. For our purposes it is sufficient to discuss only those desires which we above called particular and contingent: evaluation of different objects, the need for recognition and love, aspirations, hopes and fears and other everyday emotions and desires.

For Girard, there is an anthropological or evolutionary background to such desires. The resources of nature are always scarce and thus primitive human societies were in a constant competition for the same resources. A child learns to understand what is considered valuable through following the example of adults. This is necessary for survival, but at the same time it creates desires and, since the resources are scarce, leads to a competition among the members of the group. In this kind of situation, the one who is a model is sending two different messages to his or her rivals: "Imitate me in order that you may have a good life," and "Do not imitate me and do not reach for my good things." This is what Girard calls a "double bind." It is not a pathological phenomenon but a basic feature of human communication. Through the double bind, we both imitate others and envy them for the goods they already have.[2]

If learning, social relationships, and even most desires are created through giving and receiving models, that is, through imitation, then it is understandable that rivalry and envy are among the basic social phenomena which emerge as a result. The "double bind" described above almost necessarily creates rivalry and envy as by-products of creating the desire for objects. For Girard, this amounts to a fundamental problem underlying human violence. The mimetic desire, together with the scarcity of available resources, leads to competition, envy, and rivalry. These in turn escalate sometimes into violence.

This extremely brief sketch of Girard's elaborate theory highlights several different but related issues of "giving an example." First, the topic of mimetic desire provides a bridge between human conduct, on the one hand, and evolution and animal behavior, on the other. The paradigm of competition and the idea of learning through imitation seem to be common to all creatures. Interestingly, imitation can be described as a primitive and broad variant of giving something: animals cannot give gifts, forgive, or give thanks, but they can give and receive models from one another. Although the phenomenon of giving is semantically limited to animated beings (Introduction), it is not strictly limited to humans.

---

[2] VS 146–48.

Second, the phenomenon of competition, perhaps even a sort of market economy, becomes outlined through the concepts of mimetic desire and the double bind it creates. Competition emerges as a result of imitation. It provides the group with activities that are necessary for survival. At the same time, competition does not seem to be a very creative or innovative branch of human activity. If it is limited to a mere imitation of an already existing model, it cannot create anything new or provide any added value, but it remains a ritual repetition of past patterns of behavior.

Third, in the light of Girard's analyses the whole phenomenon of imitation appears in a negative light. It is potentially violent, it is hardly innovative, and it produces envy and rivalry as its fruits. How should a "theology of giving" evaluate this outcome? In theological tradition, imitation has received a positive appreciation. If we take Girard's challenge seriously, we probably cannot conclude simply that it is good to imitate good examples, but bad to imitate bad ones. If our learning and desire occur in a mimetic fashion as a result of an almost inevitable, even evolutionary process, then we are not free to make such enlightened judgments concerning good and bad.

Is there something similar to Girard in the theological tradition? Has the ethical point been made that you should be careful in desiring something, lest you become enmeshed in envy and rivalry through a double bind? Does anyone remind us that our very personal desires and aspirations are in reality planted into us by models? It is probable that this problematic side of "giving an example" has also received the attention of religious traditions.

One classical place to look at this phenomenon is the end of the Decalogue, the tenth commandment: "You shall not covet your neighbor's house; you shall not cover your neighbor's wife, or male or female slave, or ox, or donkey, or anything that belongs to your neighbor" (Exod 20:17, cf. Deut 5:20-21). This commandment outlines a situation in which the neighbor already possesses the resource I may desire. My neighbor is the model and I am his rival. The commandment prohibits my desire. Christian tradition has specified the nature of this desire in terms used by the apostle Paul, who in Romans 7:7 quotes this commandment. Paul employs the Greek verb *epithymein* which means desiring, which was translated into Latin as *concupiscere*. The precise meaning of the underlying Hebrew verb is to some extent debated, but generally the Hebrew word stresses the inevitable connection between desire and the corresponding action more strongly than its Greek and Latin counterparts. For our purposes, the Hebrew word may be more fitting than its translations.[3]

Whereas the other commandments of the "second table" (4–10) of the Decalogue prohibit concrete actions harming our neighbor, the situation of the tenth commandment is more complex. One common and plausible way of interpreting the tenth commandment proceeds from claiming that this commandment lays out the root causes of our sinful behavior. We are called not only to refrain from doing sin, but also from the desire that motivates such action. According to this reading, the Decalogue would resemble a house which has both a roof and a basement. The "first table" (those commandments that relate directly to God, the first three or four commandments in the differing numbering schemes) offers a view from the roof so that we can see both God and our neighbors. The tenth commandment offers a view from the basement. Under the visible structure we have the basement of desires. Although we cannot see them, they provide the foundation which, if misused or misconstrued, causes the whole house to collapse.

This interpretation probably matches with Jesus' radicalization of the law in the Sermon on the Mount (Matt 5–7) and elsewhere in the gospels. The law should be filled with an attitude of love, mercy, and *metanoia*. This attitude should penetrate the realm of desires and transform them. This is probably the most profound interpretation of the tenth commandment. In addition, one can outline a Girardian reading which is rather literal and plain. It presents the tenth commandment as a prohibition of mimetic desire.

We can illustrate this reading with the following case: You have the only donkey in our community and thus only you can visit distant places. We envy you and would also like to have a similar donkey in order to travel. In Girard's terms this is a typical double bind. You give an example of imitation but you also guard your property and do not let us take it. The possession of this resource, the donkey, signals the outcome of social competition and may lead to a violent conflict. The commandment now says that we shall not covet this donkey. The commandment probably also strengthens the eighth commandment: You

---

[3] I have not followed any particular exegetical study, although I need to mention Frank-Lothar Hossfeld, *Der Dekalog* (Freiburg: Universitätsverlag 1982) 87–140 and Cornelis Houtman, *Exodus*, vol. 3 (Leuven: Peeters, 2000) 67–71. One basic question is whether *epithymia* in Rom 7:7 captures the original meaning. In Hebrew, the emphasis may be more in possessing the objects mentioned in the commandment, although this is debated. As an actual competitive striving for possession, mimetic desire differs from the appetitive and latent *epithymia* and perhaps approaches the Hebrew meaning.

shall not steal. Thus the commandment protects the neighbor. But in addition, the prohibition of coveting concerns our relationship to ourselves. We shall not let our desire dominate us and dictate our priorities. We must abandon this heteronomy of our desire. In this sense the commandment concerns our self-relationship: we are called to abandon the slavery of mimetic desire. "You shall not covet" is a commandment of self-protection.

Thus the tenth commandment recommends disinclination and disengagement. We should liberate our desire from the trap of the model. It is our inner freedom and integrity which needs to be preserved by this commandment. In the Lutheran tradition, this type of freedom is emphasized in Luther's *The Freedom of a Christian*. Luther claims that our inner freedom is in fact a much more precious thing than external powers. If we do not have this inner freedom, we are everybody's slaves and resemble machines rather than humans. But if we have this freedom, we become truly ourselves, even if we have no external power.[4]

This reading is plain and concrete, but not without problems. It seems to affirm a strong individualism. Since binding ourselves to the examples given by others is a form of slavery and exploitation, we need to protect our integrity and find our inner freedom. The commandment prohibits coveting, but it does not say what comes after that. In Luther's *The Freedom of a Christian*, this inner freedom motivates the faithful to serve Christ and the neighbor. In a sense, the bad example becomes replaced with the good example of Christ. But how can we in practice proceed to this conclusion? Doesn't the theme of "inner freedom" rather lead to a new egoism and individualism? Is it escapist rather than liberating?

In asking these questions we approach the deep waters of Christian spirituality. On the one hand, I think that it is correct to say that the Judaeo-Christian tradition affirms a strong notion of individuality. The tenth commandment indeed encourages people to walk their own way instead of desiring the models given by neighbors. This, together with the need for "inner freedom," is a counter-cultural feature in the sense that it presents an alternative to competition and affirms diversity, whereas culture and society are for the most part concerned with common goals and team spirit.

[4] Luther's *Works*, American Edition (LW) vol. 31, 333–77, esp. 344–58.

On the other hand, one must of course remember that the tenth commandment remains only one of ten. All other commandments of the second table are concerned with justice and social well-being within the community. The communal spirit of the Decalogue does not disappear if we claim that there is an element of disengagement and withdrawal present in the last commandment. In addition, we can claim that some withdrawal and individualism may in the long run benefit the whole community, since it gives room for new thoughts and innovations.

One may also note that the "inner freedom" of Christian spirituality cannot finally be rationalized and is finally not the subject of ethics. In Eastern Orthodox spirituality, liberation from desires and earthly models of life amounts to *hesychia*, a silence and quietness in which one refuses to give sufficient explanations. In the Lutheran tradition, the discontinuity between the Law and the Gospel has traditionally been employed to express a parallel point: when we proceed from external works to inner freedom, we are no longer under the law. In making this point, Luther refers allegorically to another donkey, namely the ass of Isaac in Genesis 22:5. The ass is a servant of the law: "At the moment you are busy on earth, let the ass work, let him serve and carry the burden that has been laid upon him . . . But when you ascend into heaven, leave the ass with his burdens on earth: for the conscience has no relation to the law or to works or to earthly righteousness. Thus the ass remains in the valley; but the conscience ascends the mountain with Isaac, knowing absolutely nothing about the law or its works but looking only at the forgiveness of sins and the pure righteousness offered and given in Christ."[5] In this spirit, one may even say that the last commandment shows the way beyond commandments, from law towards gospel.

We have elaborated Girard's mimetic desire somewhat extensively in order to show that there is also in Judaeo-Christian tradition a strain which points towards renouncing the imitation of others. When we "do not covet" what our neighbor has, we can disengage ourselves towards an inner freedom. This inner freedom is a complex and difficult notion which includes risks and opportunities. It is not the whole of Christian spirituality, but only one aspect of it. We will not, however, elaborate on this notion any further. After having shown that there ought to be a balance between positive imitation on the one hand and liberating disengagement on the other, we must come back to the actual topic of this chapter.

[5] LW 26, 116; Luther, *Werke*, Weimarer Ausgabe (WA), vol. 40/1, 207–8.

Competition and Care

In imitating others, we receive desires and behavioral patterns which guide our actions and become models for others who in turn imitate us. Thus there is a circulation of models and even desires underlying the models. In this giving and receiving, some patterns may rapidly spread and become fashionable, but they may also soon be forgotten. Religious models and behavioral patterns are often characterized by their extremely long duration. Rituals and even languages that have otherwise become forgotten may continue to circulate in a religious community for centuries.

We saw that the "mimetic desire" may have problematic features and that the Judaeo-Christian tradition has also created strategies to overcome problematic mimesis. But positive imitation of saints and other exemplars has also occurred and helped to establish Christian communities with strong communal features and genuine love of neighbor. Given this, we may ask whether mimesis is so strongly linked to competition as Girard's theory seems to presuppose. In addition, we have thus far stressed the problematic features of mimetic rivalry. Can there be another mode of competition, a healthy competition?

In order to answer this question, and in order to discuss whether this is the right question to ask, we need to look at the Christian's imitation of Christ. This imitation has been regarded by Christian churches as the model of good imitation *par excellence*. Even René Girard, in spite of his emphasis on the problematic side of mimesis, approves of this "good mimesis." According to him, a fundamental change of personality becomes effective through the imitation of Christ.[6] We must immediately note that the imitation of Christ is a vast and somewhat imprecise theological topic. Protestant encyclopedias, for instance, tend to speak rather of "following Christ." At the same time they admit that this way of speaking has become prominent only since Dietrich Bonhoeffer's *Discipleship* (1937; in German *Nachfolge*, literally, "following after"), whereas imitation and conformity have been more influential terms in the Christian tradition.[7]

The historical starting-point of this terminology lies in the activity of Jesus's disciples who followed their master in a concrete and literal

[6] *The Girard Reader*, ed., James G. Williams (New York: Crossroad, 1996) 290–91.
[7] So Ulrich Luz, et al., Nachfolge Jesu, *Theologische Realenzyklopädie* 23, 678–710, here: 691. This work is also employed in the following; it contains the best overview and bibliography, including English works.

sense of the Greek verb *akoloutheô*. The more philosophical and abstract *mimeomai*, "to imitate," occurs only in Pauline letters. In 1 Corinthians 11:1 Paul asks the Corinthians to be "imitators of me, as I am of Christ"; in Ephesians 5:1 he wants the Ephesians to be "imitators of God," meaning the God in Christ (4:32). In Philippians 2:5, Paul admonishes the Philippians: "Let the same mind be in you that was in Christ Jesus." Giving an example that is to be imitated is explicitly mentioned in 2 Thessalonians 3:7, 9, but here the model is the "we" who command the Thessalonians in the name of Jesus Christ (3:6).

Existing studies in the history of doctrine often distinguish between two basic perspectives on imitation. Especially in patristic times and in Eastern Christianity, there is the imitation of Christ as the exemplary and most virtuous God-man. When the believers imitate this iconic model, they are sanctified and the image of God begins to be restored. This may even lead to *theosis*, a deification of the human being. In a particular way, this perspective concerns the ruler, an emperor or a supreme bishop, whose hierarchical position makes him a vicar and an imitator of the highest ruler, Christ Pantokrator.

The second perspective of imitation concerns the passion and humanity of Christ. We are to imitate his human journey, his suffering and struggle with the powers of evil. This form of imitation and following of Jesus has been more common in the West since medieval times. Especially Protestant textbooks give this perspective a theological priority over the patristic type, since according to them humans are not to imitate the strength and God-like features of Christ, but our engagement with Christ has to do with the cross and suffering, that is, with the example of Christ's humanity. The two modes of imitation, sanctification and suffering, have often been played against one another, but they have also been combined. It is common in mysticism and negative theology to think that our true sanctification takes place through suffering and the cross. The iconic relationship and the initial restoration of the image of God does not take place in terms of visible glory, but through the cross.

For our purposes it is not necessary to enter this discussion in more detail. Our study is concerned with a more general point: Both the perspective of iconic sanctification and the perspective of following the passion of Jesus are connected in their view of struggle. The model, Jesus Christ, overcomes evil. He may be portrayed as the champion of this struggle or as a suffering servant who is to be followed in the most difficult moment of his battle. In both perspectives, however, it is finally the one who overcomes, *Christus victor,* who serves as the model. Both the mode of glory and the mode of suffering employ this model of *Christus victor.*

This way of speaking of Christ who overcomes evil is classical and prominent. It cannot be neglected in orthodox theology. For our initial question, however, *Christus victor* with all its implications is a many-sided topic. The Christ thus imitated is depicted in images of competition and warfare. In the one perspective you feel yourself overcome by the devil and temptation, or at least by the disappointments of the world. Then you find consolation in the suffering of Christ. Or you aspire to the good and virtuous life, having the God-man as an iconic picture of perfection before you. This is probably the "healthy competition" that our initial question was seeking. It is healthy in the sense that you are not striving to harm your neighbor but your competition is a spiritual struggle or a spiritual exercise in which you are trained in order that you may overcome the evil.

But is this the whole story of our chapter, the fundamental meaning of "giving an example" in Christianity? We have argued that the imitation of Christ offers this meaning *par excellence,* and that the two historical perspectives on this imitation, sanctification and suffering, are united in their depicting the spiritual life of a Christian as a warfare in which we imitate the finally victorious struggle of Christ against the powers of evil. This seems to be the fundamental meaning. But then the spiritual life of imitation would indeed be rather close to the problematic side of mimetic desire that Girard has outlined. In the imitation of Christ we are, according to this result, elevated from the evolutionary struggle to a spiritual struggle.

The spiritual struggle is nonviolent in the sense that it does not involve a physical combat against your neighbor. But it remains bound to the imagery of warfare and competition. Moreover, it seems to be a rather individualistic and even egoistic way of following an example. In both modes of this imitation, followers are concerned with their own steadfast aspiration. The perspective of the neighbor does not come into focus. This is understandable, since the very language of competition and struggle focuses on one's own survival, be it evolutionary or spiritual. But there seems to be a problem in that the model of *Christus victor* has as its mimetic counterpart *homo militans,* the fighting and competitive human person.

My claim is that this is not a balanced or a theologically sufficient view of Christian imitation. There is in fact another christological model which has not been adequately distinguished in theological textbooks. This is basically the model of Christ as Good Samaritan, as healer and caretaker of the needs of the others. This is the Christ who offers poietic love in terms of the Golden Rule (ch. 2), that is, who does not measure humans by their works but who meets their needs. It is the diaconic Christ who does not think of his own aspiration and struggle but who gives to others. This Christ says that giving food, drink, and clothing, taking care of other people and visiting them (Matt 25:35-40), is the most important thing to do.

I will label this model as *Christus medicus*, with an awareness that it is not only the medical dimension that is at stake here, but the whole field of caretaking and service. Of course, *Christus medicus* is also concerned with redemption and salvation, as the very word "salvation" points out. But in the context of imitation, I will not discuss the salvific meaning, but only the diaconic Christ as example. The imitation of this model is visible, for example, in the field of the "cure of the souls," in Greek *therapeia tês psykhês*, in Latin *cura animarum*. The Latin and Greek phrases are important since they denote an important differentiation of this imitation in East and West. The Greek *therapeia*, which connects Jesus' work as healer with Hellenistic medical and philosophical therapy, amounts first to the moderation of passions and desires in monastic settings, and later to the development of spiritual guidance in the Orthodox tradition, of which the collection *Philokalia* is the best-known example.[8] As spiritual guidance, this mode of medical imitation is dialogical and private. It probably stresses more the dialogical meaning, the *communio*, of interhuman communication (introduction).

The Latin *cura*, although a translation from its Greek counterpart, is not only or even predominantly medical, but it comprehends all caretaking and administration. In keeping with this broad general meaning, the *cura animarum* of Western Christianity involved teaching, administration, and also diaconic and social work. Thus it became almost identical with general pastoral and parish work, comprising both witness and service. This mode of imitation developed into an administrative responsibility and care for the local and universal church. In so doing, it probably emphasizes more the proclamatory side, the

---

[8] See e.g. *Philokalia: The Complete Text,* vol. 1–4, ed. Kallistos Ware, et al. (London: Faber & Faber, 1981). For the history of the notion *cura animarum*, see Gerhard Ebeling, "Luthers Gebrauch der Wortfamilie 'Seelsorge'," in *Lutherjahrbuch* 61, 1994, 7–44. The larger background of this phenomenon is found in Hellenism, see e.g. Martha Nussbaum, *The Therapy of Desire* (Princeton: Princeton University Press, 1994).

munus, of human communication (Introduction). We will not here, however, play the Western and the Eastern models against each others, but see them both in terms of service to other. Both administration and therapy can serve the well-being of one's neighbors.

The diaconic model of *Christus medicus* has thus as its mimetic counterpart *homo curator*, a human person who exercises poietic love towards others in healing, serving, and administering to their needs. Of course this altruistic side is not totally missing in the portrayal of the imitation of Christ in the textbooks. Sometimes it appears in the context of either sanctification or suffering. My claim is, however, that altruistic service should be clearly distinguished from these two perspectives of struggle and be understood as a different basic model of imitation. It is heuristically important to make a clear conceptual distinction between the two models of *Christus victor* and *Christus medicus*. Through this distinction the problems of competitive mimesis and the relative autonomy of altruistic mimesis can be adequately understood.

Whereas the first mimesis is able to portray steadfastness and aspiration, virtues that are born in a healthy competition but remain vulnerable to individualism, the second mimesis portrays poietic love and altruism. In doing so it highlights some themes which we have identified already in the earlier chapters of this book: the poietic account of the golden rule (ch. 2), forgiveness as mercy towards others (ch. 3), and the "spiritual sacrifice" of giving oneself for the sake of others (ch. 4). Thus the second mimesis gives an example of true giving. Christ is portrayed as a model of giving, and we are called to follow this example of true giving and self-giving.

In this way, *homo curator* brings together many themes of this book. It portrays a Christian anthropology in terms of giving and self-giving. It may also serve as an ethical application of the theology of giving: we are to follow Christ not only in our personal aspiration and struggle, but also, and perhaps in particular, in our service to our neighbors. We must again stress that our mimetic approach first brings together two features which textbooks often separate, namely the imitation of both glory and tribulation. In both perspectives, *Christus victor* is imitated by *homo militans*. Second, our approach identifies and distinguishes another mimesis, which is not competitive or aspiring, but altruistic: in this mimesis, *Christus medicus* is being followed by *homo curator*. Our distinction emphasizes that the two forms of Christian mimesis go in opposite directions: the first one is formative and supportive, whereas the second is outpouring and distributive.

We have thus captured the imitation of Christ in a richer fashion: the mimesis it recommends is not only a Girardian mimetic desire linked with competition. It is also that, but in addition we have identified an altruistic mode of mimesis in which Christ appears as healer and the human person as caretaker. We may note in passing that this second mimesis is perhaps no less evolutionary than the first one, since biological nature is not only a model of violence and competition, but also a model of such ecological cooperation which does not waste resources to pointless violence. In this sense, the phenomena of giving and caretaking are not absent from biological nature.[9]

Since our main topic is the "theology of giving," it is perhaps obvious that this second mimesis appears in a more positive light than the first one. In general, however, my claim and my discussion have tried to show that the first mimesis and the model of *Christus victor* are insufficient, not that they are wrong. Moreover, the conceptual opposition between aspiring and altruistic mimesis does not mean that they would exclude each other in concrete life. On the contrary, they may strengthen one another in everyday surroundings. In order to establish a hospital for poor people, you need a strong character so that you can struggle your way through practical difficulties. And vice versa, if you must strive through hardships and suffering in your own life, you may develop a capacity to understand and alleviate your neighbor's difficulties as well. Of course, these two dimensions neither logically imply nor exclude each other in any way. They may, however, complement each other in concrete situations. In this sense, *homo militans* can be as positive a trait of character as *homo curator*.

Our discussion has lead to the following result: Christ can be called a model in two paradigmatic ways, as *victor* and as *medicus*. Christ approaches us in both these exemplary forms. In following the example of Christ, the human being can emphasize aspiration and suffering *(militans),* but also altruistic caretaking and giving *(curator).* These different arts of mimesis are complementary. In addition, one has to realize the importance of human disengagement: we are not called to follow models always and everywhere, but need also time and opportunity to set our desires aside. This withdrawal from earthly

[9] This point is often made by contemporary population ecology. For the sake of survival, all populations optimize their use of energy, and for this purpose peaceful behavior and cooperation is normally more successful than mutual struggle. Thus natural selection does not recommend competitive violence but favors peacebuilding mechanisms.

activities is an inherent factor of Christian spirituality; it is connected with the tenth commandment.

Given this picture, we may ask whether there is in Christian theology a moment of Christ's disengagement or perhaps a mode in which Christ does not serve as example. The question is tricky and ambiguous. This mode is not needed for the sake of symmetry. Nor is it meant that God would need a piety that would resemble human spirituality. We rather ask whether there is a dimension of partiality and impartiality, or a polarity of love and justice in God. As a model of imitation, Christ's love and engagement for all people is already emphasized. Imitation is a picture of closeness to God. Nevertheless, picturing God's justice and impartiality perhaps needs a moment or a conceptual picture in which God remains distant and is not connected through any exemplary mode with humans.

In Christian tradition, the picture of *Christus iudex*, that is, of Christ who will come to judge the living and the dead, has served as such a conceptual picture. A judge must serve justice and be impartial. In order to give fair judgments, one has to be disengaged from the persons who are to be judged. The judge is in the service of truth, and in this service the judge must not be attached to the people who are to be judged.

In a sense, there is an interesting parallel, though neither an imitation nor a symmetry, between Christ as judge and the Christian person as disengaged and free, as *homo liber*. As judge, Christ remains in the service of truth. Human persons who in their disengagement exercise their inner freedom and the particular kind of spirituality involved in it, are through this freedom also in the service of truth, or at least of impartiality and fairness. The human persons in question are scrutinizing their motives and try not to be bound to any act of coveting or desiring which the models around them suggest. *Homo liber* does not judge others, but performs instead a sort of self-examination or even self-judgment.

The two modes of disengagement are not connected with each other by imitation. *Homo liber* does not follow *Christus iudex*. There is rather a conscious opposition between the two modes, since Christ judges the living and the dead, whereas the human person is called to self-examination. In a way, however, the two modes represent a middle point or at least a neutral point from which one can either proceed towards competitive aspiration and struggle (*Christus victor, homo militans*) or towards poietic care for your neighbors (*Christus medicus, homo curator*).

This mode of disengagement provides a stop or a crossing in which one must examine which mode of mimesis, or which combination of competition and care, would be adequate in the situation at hand. The point of departure, the disengagement of *homo liber*, serves the finding of one's personal way of life, although the point in itself cannot be the way. Figuratively speaking, the totality of imitation proceeds in a triangle: on the top you have the disengagement of *homo liber*, whereas the two lower angles represent the modes of competition *(militans)* and care *(curator)*. Proceeding from the top angle, one must in a sense choose between two different lines. At the same time, the two mimetic angles are also connected with each other and in reality the engaging person often exercises both competition and care.

We will not, however, carry this kind of speculative systematics any further. We have only outlined a compact view of the phenomenon of "giving an example" in Christianity. Every single element in this view is traditional, but the organization of them in this fashion is, as far as I can see, an innovation. In outlining this innovative organization two aims have been followed: first, we have taken seriously René Girard's theory of mimetic desire but at the same time argued that the scale of positive imitation is broader than in Girard's theory. Second, concerning the imitation of Christ we have argued that the basic opposition between cross and glory represents only one side of the complex phenomenon of imitation. A more fundamental opposition occurs between competitive following and altruistic care.

Being Gifted

When you are forgiven, you receive positive gifts of God (ch. 3). When you receive the Eucharist, you are first and foremost given a spiritual nourishment, a sacramental gift (ch. 4). When you follow Christ and let this imitation have an effect, you may become Christlike in some fashion (ch. 5). All these theological realities express gifts that are received by Christians. The believer is being gifted when he or she receives the gifts in question.

At this point, one may easily engage in a long debate on the more precise specification of the nature of the gifts received. Are they to be understood as ontological changes, or changes in our personal attitudes, or perhaps moral changes? Or are they more like charisms, gifts of grace which endow the person with new abilities? Such debates have shaped dogmatic textbooks and ecumenical debates. They also have very concrete manifestations in congregations discussing sanctification and the various charisms. Many important Christian denominations (for example, Pentecostals) emphasize the visible signs of such changes and claim that we must witness through charisms which we can experience and make manifest.

Since this book is not about ontology or dogmatics in general, I cannot enter these debates, although I consider them to be highly relevant for Christian self-understanding. They deserve an extensive treatment which would easily cover another book or a whole series of books. But I will not discuss ontology, sanctification, or the theology of charisms. Instead, I will focus on a related topic that I regard as a small but important prerequisite for any larger debate. I will focus on the meaning of the phrase "being gifted" as it is understood in common language, philosophy, and theology. In other words, I will briefly elaborate on the issue of talents.

The phrase "being gifted" is many-sided and complex. When teachers or other people say today that somebody is gifted, they do not mean that the talents in question would have literally come from some external source or giver. On the contrary, the phrase is often employed in order to say the opposite, that somebody is inherently bright, that he or she possesses some valuable properties from the beginning. The gift has not been given by the teacher, but it is already there when the school begins its work. A talent needs education and nurture, but we do not normally think that the notion of talents involves a transfer of something to an ordinary person so that the person from a certain point on can be called "gifted." On the contrary, when we say that this child is gifted, we mean that the child from the beginning possesses something and therefore does not need so much teacher-given training as other children. Being gifted is presented as an autonomous or inherent feature of the person.

While the phrase "being gifted" in this way downplays the aspect of an external giver, it highlights another aspect of the classical gift at the same time. A gift is neither earned through hard work nor is it a reward for your activity. A gift comes to you, or exists in you, as a free gift. A child who without training learns to read at the age of four is gifted in this sense. The child possesses "a gift" which allows for rapid development of new skills. This gift may be of genetic or biological origin, but it is not achieved. The child simply has it.

This second aspect of "being gifted" resembles some classical features of the theological gift. If the first aspect showed a certain autonomy of being gifted, the second aspect displays a heteronomy. The gift in question is heteronomous in the sense that we cannot control and manipulate it. It is not of our doing that this child is so clever. It would also be strange to say that the child himself or herself has caused this state of affairs. The child in question enjoys these capacities without any subjective effort. The gifts are in some metaphorical sense "put into" the child by some external but anonymous giver, and in this metaphorical sense they are heteronomous.

Our contemporary way of speaking about "being gifted" thus employs a dialectic between autonomy and heteronomy. This dialectic resembles, but is not identical with, other aporias or dialectical relationships we have observed in previous chapters. A gifted person has received a gift which, by definition, is not his or her own achievement. At the same time, the state of being gifted is an inherent feature and autonomous resource of this person. We need not develop this dialectic into a Derrida-like aporia of the gift (ch. 1), but can be content with just observing it.

This dialectic is non-theological and can be employed in general discussions concerning education, pedagogy, and the interplay of hereditary and learned features of human conduct. It has, however, a theological background which may illustrate why this dialectic still shapes our understanding of "being gifted." We will therefore look at this background in more detail.

One starting-point for this dialectic can be seen in the contrast between virtues and gifts. For Aristotle and Thomas Aquinas, virtues emerge as a result of exercise and learning. In his *Summa theologiae* (= Sth, II/1 q68 a1r) , Thomas remarks that unlike virtues, gifts are directly given or infused into us. Thomas has in mind the "seven gifts of the Holy Spirit," (Isa 11:2) that in principle summarize the ways human beings can be gifted. Because of the comprehensive character of the seven gifts what is said about them pertains to human giftedness in general.

For Thomas, the seven are "spirits" which are "in us by divine inspiration" (Sth II/1 q68 a1r). Inspiration is a motion coming from outside; thus it is the extrinsic principle of human movement, namely, God as Spirit. The virtues form the human person as she is driven by her intrinsic principle, human reason. The gifts dispose humans to be moved by the extrinsic principle, God, and they are themselves infused into us by God. The gifts perfect humans for acts higher than the acts of virtue (Sth II/1 q68 a1r).

The virtues and the gifts refer to the same thing in humans, namely human movement, as its intrinsic and extrinsic disposition. Human action is therefore both autonomous and heteronomous. The gifts highlight the heteronomous reality. At the same time they are, as dispositions, human properties which go together with the intrinsic, reason-based virtues. Although Thomas in this way built a gift-based action theory on top of Aristotle's virtue-based ethics, he remarks that even Aristotle saw the necessity of this super-virtuous or heteronomous aspect of action when in the *Nicomachean Ethics* (1145a15-20) Aristotle speaks of the so-called heroic virtue which is a divine principle in humans (Sth II/1 q68 a1 ad1).

For Thomas, the gifts are higher than normal virtues, but lower than the so-called theological virtues of faith, hope, and charity (Sth II/1 q68 a8). He develops a complex interplay between virtues and gifts which together, through this interaction, aim at the perfection of humans. We need not go more deeply into this interplay, but it is important to see in what sense the gifts are heteronomous: they are given through inspiration and refer to the extrinsic principle of movement. In concrete human action, however, gifts go together with the intrinsic and autonomous virtues, especially since the theological virtues are also infused by God: "There is no reason why that which comes from another as a gift should not perfect a person for right action; especially since we said above that certain virtues are infused into us by God" (Sth II/1 q68 a1r).

In this sense, the educational value of virtues and gifts is similar: both dispose and prepare a person for right conduct. In a concrete situation it is difficult to distinguish whether one acts in an excellent way as a result of being gifted or as a result of hard work and exercise. Interestingly, however, the distinction between achieved and non-achieved features of human conduct has remained relevant for behavioral sciences.

The Lutheran Reformation was critical of virtue ethics since it was thought to lead to a theologically mistaken self-righteousness. We should not rely on our own virtue and practice, but remain faithful to God's word. In this sense, heteronomy overruled autonomy. At the same time, Lutherans were very interested in schools and education. Luther's companion Philip Melanchthon wrote new textbooks in which he outlined a distinctive profile for Lutheran educational work. Since Melanchthon's textbooks remained influential in the European universities across confessional boundaries for centuries, their view of heteronomous gift deserves to be given some attention.

On the one hand, Melanchthon rescues the old university disciplines through saying that they should be dealt with in terms of natural reason and the law. At the same time, however, he wants to preserve the theocentric and gift-oriented profile of the Lutheran Reformation through insisting that in reality God has given us everything. Therefore, philosophy and natural knowledge, *notitiae*, are fundamentally to be regarded as divinely given notions impressed upon our souls (*notitiae impressae animis divinitus*). Even philosophical virtues (for example, justice) emerge from notions given through God (*ex notitiis de Deo*).[10]

As we saw, Thomas only mentions in passing Aristotle's idea of "heroic virtue." In Melanchthon, as with many other early Lutheran writers,[11] this topic receives significant attention as a paradigmatic case of the interplay between divine gift and human action. This is interesting already for the historical reason that in Catholicism heroic virtue has remained a criterion for declaring persons to be saints. The Reformation abandoned the veneration of saints, but at the same time showed a great interest in the notion of heroism. In my view, this was because the Reformers wanted to develop and refine the ethics of the gift and the understanding of humans as "being gifted."

Melanchthon often quotes Cicero's dictum (*De nat. deor.* 2,66) that "nobody becomes a great man without divine inspiration." Different people have different natural capacities that allow for one person to become a great musician, while others may become extraordinary mathematicians or are distinguished by their magnificent courage. These gifts are for Melanchthon natural in the sense of "natural notions," which means that they are not learned but *a priori* given by God to the person in question. Divine inspiration is thus at work in extraordinary musicians, mathematicians, and soldiers.

Although this view of gifts probably has received something from medieval Thomist discussion, it is much more individualistic than the Aristotelian-Thomist synthesis of the gift. For Melanchthon, God has distributed various gifts among human beings in a way which may be

---

[10] See e.g. Melanchthon, "Philosophiae moralis epitomes," in *Werke, Studienausgabe*, Bd. 3 (Gütersloh: Gerd Mohn, 198–200). I follow the interpretations given in more detail in Risto Saarinen, "Melanchthons Ethik zwischen Tugend und Begabung," in *Melanchthon*, ed., Walter Sparn (Erlangen: Universitätsbibliothek, 1998) 75–94 and Günter Frank, *Melanchthons Theologische Philosophie* (Leipzig: Benno, 1995).

[11] For this and the following, see Saarinen 1998 and the materials presented in Risto Saarinen, Virtus heroica, *Archiv für Begriffsgeschichte* 33, 1990 96–114.

called democratic but also highly accidental and elitist. It is democratic in the sense that anybody may have a rare gift, but also accidental and elitist in the sense that the natural notions and gifts are unequally distributed. Early Lutheran textbooks of ethics discuss extensively the range and quality of such divine gifts.[12] This individualistic analysis was probably also relevant for educational purposes. Melanchthon's view of highly different human abilities allowed teachers to treat their pupils individually, while also saying that all are fundamentally equal in the sense that these abilities are finally gifts given by God, not human achievements.

In these ways the Lutheran Reformation probably received something from the individualism of the Renaissance and Humanism. It also paved the way for the concept of genius, which became prominent later in the Enlightenment. In an interesting manner, natural talent here coincides with divine gift. Both denote an alternative to the ethics of virtue and declare that the foundation of excellence lies not only in hard work, but also on an already existing talent. This view clearly provides both opportunities and dangers. It may lead to the flourishing of an individual, but also to a neglect of communal virtues. We cannot here discuss the decline of virtue ethics in the sixteenth century, as provocatively described by Alasdair MacIntyre and others, but we must briefly note that this decline was counteracted by an emphasis on the ethics of the gift.[13]

What is interesting for us in this historical development is not its elitism and alleged individualism, but rather the fact that it approaches our late modern ways of speaking. "Being gifted" is almost inevitably an elitist notion, because it separates the person in question from others to whom a comparison is made. If this goes together with an emphasis on the precious autonomy of a person's talents, then we approach an educational view that is not only elitist, but even discriminatory. Seeing the gift as a precious quality of the pupil, perhaps caused by extraordinary genetic combinations but nevertheless an autonomous property and resource, approaches an ideology in which human beings become material for developing superhuman qualities. In the era of genetic engineering and hard competition, this view may lead not only to discrimination against others, but also to the exploitation of the gifted person in question.

---

[12] Saarinen 1990, 103–111; 1998, 90–94.
[13] See Alasdair MacIntyre, *After Virtue*, 2nd ed. (London: Duckworth, 1985).

In speaking of giftedness and the gift, heteronomy keeps the necessary balance. The point of "inspiration," so emphatically made by both Thomas Aquinas and Philip Melanchthon, does not refer to the artist's own creativity, but to his or her final dependence on the external giver. In the Christian era, this giver was considered to be the Holy Spirit. But probably today even an atheist can meaningfully say that his or her inspiration comes from outside. The artist may mean that she is dependent on (1) some gift within her, or that (2) she needs to relate to an external object and receive it, or, quite like Thomas, that (1) and (2) are both needed as the ability to receive and the external giver. This non-theistic heteronomy is not related to faith, but it is needed in order to preserve humility and openness.

Thus both a Christian and a non-theistic artist can refer to inspiration in a similar manner. This observation can perhaps be explained to some extent with the help of Jean-Luc Marion's view of givenness (ch. 1). We saw that Marion can "bracket" both the giver and the gift and claim that the truth of the gift appears in the very givenness of our phenomenological reality. For him, it is the openness and the "givability" of the phenomena which allow for seeing reality in terms of self-giving. This ethos, which does not need any explicit theology, resembles artistic humility and openness with regard to the necessity of extrinsic inspiration.

If humility and openness can be preserved through an emphasis on the heteronomy of "being gifted," then the problems of elitism and discrimination appear less virulent. They will probably not disappear completely, since the very dialectic of "being gifted" requires autonomy, self-preservation, and freedom. In a complex manner, the state of "being gifted" presupposes both engagement with the gift at hand and disengagement from the group around the person. Of course, this disengagement should not mean neglect or arrogance. We may rather say that the autonomy of the gift creates an individuation of the gifted person, and this individuation must be preserved over against the group.

This is not only the hero's perspective; things look surprisingly similar from the side of the community. One standard question in early Lutheran ethical texts is whether we should imitate exceptional persons. The standard answer is negative. Even if they were models of heroic virtue and divine gifts, the very fact that their behavior is exceptional warns us from following them. Melanchthon says that they are *extra regulam,* outside the rule to be followed in everyday life.[14] Saints

---

[14] Melanchthon, *Werke, Bd. 3*, 195.

and heroes are distinguished by their loneliness. They give an example in a very qualified sense.

Finally, I repeat that in describing the dialectic of heteronomy and autonomy we have not made any really "ontological" commitments. We have not described the "being" presupposed in someone's being gifted. The two topics of this chapter, imitation and talents, have to do more with ethics and human conduct than with metaphysics and being. Another reason for our neglect of ontology might be that the prerequisites outlined here are rather independent of the ontological approach chosen by dogmatic theologians. Thomas Aquinas, Philip Melanchthon, contemporary educationalists, and genetic engineers have probably very different ontologies. But their introductory problem, whether something is achieved or simply "given" to the person, seems to be surprisingly similar, irrespective of their other scientific and religious commitments.

6

Ecumenical Sharing

We began the first chapter of our study with some thoughts concerning ecumenical theology, in particular the issue of reception. In chapters 1 to 5 occasional remarks were made on ecumenism, but no explicit ecumenical theology was developed. Certainly, our concentration on such confessionally prominent theologians as Anselm of Canterbury, Thomas Aquinas, Martin Luther, and Philip Melanchthon kept the ecumenical situation in mind. Moreover, topics like forgiveness and eucharistic sacrifice are among the classical ecumenical issues between Protestants and Roman Catholics. But our thematic concentration focused on the issues themselves, not on their ecumenical significance.

In this last chapter we will have a closer look at the ecumenical significance of our discussion. We will use materials from chapters 1 to 5, but will at the same time present more than a summary of our results. This "more" is worked out with the help of ecumenical examples and problems. We will ask in what sense their treatment can be enriched through our "theology of giving" as outlined in chapters 1 to 5.

At the end of chapter 1, we briefly presented a particular Anglican-Roman Catholic ecumenical text, *The Gift of Authority*, and discussed how its concept of gift must be understood in view of the twentieth-century conceptual refinement. We noted the document's uncritical use of the concept: offering the gift of papacy to another church does not appear as a free and uninterested gift, but rather as a Trojan horse which masks self-interest to look like a gift. After discussing the classical theological discussions relating to giving and the gift in chapters 2 to 5, we are now in the position to ask whether similar conscious and unconscious maskings of the gift characterize the whole Western theological tradition.

In my view, this is not the case. On the contrary, we have noted a remarkable conceptual sophistication and awareness of the many-sided phenomenon of giving during the history of theology. The twentieth-century refinement of the gift in anthropology and in philosophy was in many ways anticipated in theology. Already the New Testament verbs *didômi*, "to give," and *paradidômi*, "to hand over," develop a dynamic in which the circulation of giving (in John 2) and the "bracketing" of the giver and receiver (*paradidômi* in early passion narratives) witness to a theological differentiation. Both the asymmetrical mutuality of giving and receiving and the phenomenon of "misrecognizing" the bracketed giver and receiver are present in biblical narratives.

Especially through the writings of Augustine, Anselm of Canterbury, and Thomas Aquinas, a grammar of human giving, offering, and sacrificing emerges in which a four-place relation among (1) the giver, (2) the gift, (3) the recipient, and (4) the beneficiary is consciously employed. With the help of this grammar, one can construe elaborate theories of redemption and eucharistic sacrifice (ch. 4). The Lutheran Reformation to an extent adopted this grammar, but also criticized heavily some of its theological placeholders, especially the figure in which humans give something to God in order that other humans may benefit from this act.

As a result of this criticism and through a concentration on biblical notions of giving and poietic doing (*poieô, poiêsis*), Martin Luther developed a consistent theology of theocentric giving. In Luther's theology, the model of God's outpouring agape becomes a model for Christian love of the neighbor (ch. 2). The figure of divine self-giving is prominent in this model, as it becomes applied to the Lutheran understanding of the Eucharist as a "spiritual sacrifice" in which people offer themselves in service of their neighbors (ch. 4). Concerning the theology of forgiveness, Lutheran tradition has often understood forgiveness not as gift, but as favor and mercy. Here the Lutheran tradition has perhaps lost something. In critical discussion with Søren Kierkegaard and John Milbank, our study argues that God's favor and gift need not be played against one another if forgiveness is understood as "negative giving" (ch. 3). When we combine positive and negative giving with another dimension, that of remembering and forgetting, we may gain a concept of forgiveness that embraces the positive gift. This concept, as constructed in ch. 3, receives something from Luther and Kierkegaard, but more importantly it reflects the New Testament metaphors of release, liberation, and cleansing and shows in what sense the contemporary churches' different emphases can be reconciled.

The Perspective of the Giver

This brief historical outline of our results shows that the theological tradition understands giving and its various sub-species in a highly differentiated manner. For this reason, it has not been our aim to claim that the twentieth-century philosophical discussion on the gift should be understood as a new challenge to theology. In discussing the gift with contemporary philosophy, theology is not facing new challenges or new frontiers, but rather revitalizing its old resources. In chapters 2 to 5, we have attempted at such a revitalization of some classical theological topics.

At the same time, however, the ecumenical discussion is not very well aware of the many faces of the gift. In discussing reception, the gift of salvation, and the exchange of gifts in general, ecumenists have not only neglected contemporary discussions but also their own theological traditions. Ecumenical documents sometimes present "gift exchange" as a completely harmless and altruistic phenomenon. Sometimes they are playing God's favor and gift, or forgiveness and the gift, against one another instead of joining them. On still other occasions, ecumenical texts understand the gift as a completely unilateral or monergistic movement which need not be concerned with the underlying pre-conditions of the recipient.[1] These simplifications are perhaps necessary in short texts. At the same time, however, they remain in need of more elaboration, not only to meet the standards of contemporary philosophical refinement and the semantics of our everyday language, but above all to match the doctrinal positions of classical theology. Our study has attempted to do some of this necessary elaboration.

In the Introduction we suggested that ecumenical theology, perhaps even Western theology in general, should for a while set aside its "receiver-oriented" perspective and look at the issues from the

---

[1] See the texts given by Margaret O'Gara, *The Ecumenical Gift Exchange* (Collegeville: Liturgical Press, 1998) esp. vii–viii, 35–38, and The Joint Declaration on the Doctrine of Justification, in *Growth in Agreement,* vol 2, eds., Harding Meyer et al. (Grand Rapids: Eerdmans, 1998) 566–82, esp. § 22–24 (favor, forgiveness and the gift), 17, 25 (monergy of the gift).

perspective of the giver. We claimed that, in a somewhat paradoxical manner, the giver-oriented perspective allows us to see better the inherent activity of the recipient. It probably also allows us to see better the limits of unilateral or monergistic giving.

The limits become visible when we speak of human beings giving gifts to their neighbors. From the receiver-oriented perspective, the recipient does not loose anything but gains the gift at hand. Moreover, the gift represents the otherness of the giver in the following sense: I give you this item which comes from my peculiar tradition, and you are glad to have that in addition to your old things. This perspective, in which the gift appears as a souvenir reminding us of the otherness of the giver, is an important but nevertheless very limited and even misleading perspective. From the perspective of the giver things look different. In giving some item as reminder, the giver should consider whether a problematic obligation is being imposed on the recipient. A considerate giver does not simply distribute his own favorite items to others, but he considers what others may need and what they would like to have. A giver is supposed to consider the feelings of the recipient in choosing the gift.

From the giver-oriented perspective, many contemporary ecumenical interpretations of gift exchange seem to lack this consideration. Let us consider what the "souvenir model" of the gift would imply in relationships among the churches. It is presupposed that each community of faith has its own peculiar charisms and gifts which others might not have. In an exchange of gifts, they distribute their own specificities to others. Thus Roman Catholics would like to give papacy to all other churches, whereas Pentecostals would like to see that every church practices speaking in tongues. But this is clearly a distorted picture of "gift exchange." In giving gifts, the givers should not propagate their peculiarities, but the very idea of the gift presupposes freedom and considerate behavior. If I have papacy and you don't, it does not mean that my best gift to you would be papacy. Perhaps you lack something else and would really need it. You may even think that as a considerate giver I would possess so much empathy or skill in applying the golden rule of reciprocity that I can give you what you really need. In aid programs, for instance, such considerations play a major role. In ecumenical exchange, however, they are not given much attention.

It seems that the ecumenical movement has confused two paradigms with each other, namely the paradigm of gift exchange on the one hand and the Pauline picture of one body and many members on the other. The Pauline picture is not a picture of gift exchange. The hand is not proposing to other members that everybody should become manual, nor the mouth that other members should become oral. Rather, each member preserves the particular gifts it has. At the same time, they serve each other with this gift and share the benefits achieved through using the particular gifts. In this sharing, it is not the gifts that are shared, but rather the benefits or the service.

The interplay of the two paradigms is complex and it is easy to confuse them. To illustrate this, let us look at the following deduction. We claim that (1) each ecclesial communion should have all spiritual gifts, and in addition that (2) all differences among the communions are in reality peculiar spiritual gifts. From (1) and (2) it logically follows that (3) you should adopt all specifities of my tradition. The deduction is persuasive, since the two premises (1,2) look generous and liberal and it is easy to embrace them. But the logical conclusion (3) means that I should impose everything I have on you, which is a paternalistic and manipulative strategy of spreading one's own truth. The spirit of (3) thus differs radically from the spirit of (1) and (2). At the same time, however, (3) logically follows from (1) and (2).

In my view, this deduction can be called an "ecumenical fallacy." The problem lies in the premises: there is no reason why all churches should have exactly the same gifts, or that one church should have all gifts. Such an omnipotence of one member actually distorts the Pauline picture of body and members. Only if we confuse the Pauline picture of different members with the paradigm of "gift exchange," are we persuaded to adopt both (1) and (2).

Concerning the ecumenically fruitful gift exchange, our study emphasizes that the nature of this exchange should be carefully explained. In the Introduction we quoted the Second Vatican Council document *Lumen gentium* which says that "each part contributes its own gifts to other parts and to the whole Church, so that the whole and each of the parts are strengthened by the common sharing of all things." A bit later the document mentions the Pauline picture of "diversity among its [the church's] members" and then quotes 1 Peter 4:10: "according to the gift that each has received, administer *(diakonountes)* it to one another."[2]

[2] Lumen gentium 13, in *Vatican Council II: The Conciliar and Post-Conciliar Documents*, ed., Austin Flannery (Boston: St. Paul Editions, 1988) 364–65.

This dense passage of *Lumen gentium* brings many things together. 1 Peter 4:10 speaks of diaconic service: "serve one another with whatever gift each of you has received" in the wording of the *New Revised Standard Version*. Strictly speaking, the verse does not speak of an exchange of gifts, but says that we are all charismatic people who should serve one another with our own gifts. Each individual gift benefits everyone but gifts *per se* are not exchanged. Even the wording "administer it to one another" seems to go too far, because it is diaconic service which is meant here. The "Petrine picture" of 1 Peter 4:10 is therefore very close to what we have called the Pauline picture. Both pictures recommend sharing and service, but also presuppose that there is a diversity of gifts that remains in the community, since the charisms are not exchanged.

In the Introduction, following common usage, we called this section of *Lumen gentium* a description of "gift exchange." After this closer look, however, we probably have to make a difference between "ecumenical sharing" and "the exchange of gifts." Sharing takes place within the frames of the Pauline picture in which various members serve and benefit one another. An exchange of gifts in the strict sense breaks the conceptual frame of the Pauline picture and endows the individual members with genuinely new gifts. Of course, real gift exchange also happens among the churches and in many cases it can be recommended. Yves Congar's description of reception (Introduction) entails a view in which a gift is received in the sense of a genuine exchange. A church is renewed as a result of receiving new gifts, and especially from the perspective of the recipient such renewal is often welcome, as studies on reception have shown.

But from the perspective of the giver one can, and must, add other qualifications. There is probably no compelling theological reason to go beyond the Pauline (or Petrine) picture. I probably have no duty to give my specifities to you as "gift," nor have you any duty to receive them. We are called to exercise ecumenical sharing in terms of the Pauline paradigm and thus there is a compelling reason for sharing with one another and for serving and benefiting our neighbors. But ecumenical gift exchange is something different. It resembles a free enterprise: for the renewal of churches it is good to receive new gifts, but there is no necessity or duty involved in this process of reception. On the contrary, mutual freedom is embedded in the very notion of the gift.

The exchange of gifts is thus a process which presupposes great freedom for both participants. It does not amount to saying that we are called to give our own specifities to our neighbors. The idea of poietic giving (ch. 2) requires that we give what others need, not what we would like to propagate or administer to them. Thus we see that the concept of gift exchange is complex, especially when we outline it from the giver-oriented perspective. Ecumenical dialogues cannot refer to gift exchange as a mere slogan, but they must have a clear understanding of what particular gifts this exchange involves and how they are given and received.

Finally, we must add one more dimension, since we have above dealt more or less only with interhuman giving. Theologically speaking, it is God who first gives everything to us as a gift. *Lumen gentium* clearly follows this sequence of circulation: God gives to us, we give to our neighbors. Some may argue that because God has first given us a particular gift, for instance papacy or speaking in tongues, we now have an obligation to spread this gift further and in this sense "administer it to one another." In one sense this is true, but in my view this concerns more the theology of mission and evangelization than the theology of giving and the gift. The concept of gift evokes that of obligation only reluctantly. 1 Peter 4:10 does not prescribe any such obligation, since its exhortation relates to mutual service.

Moreover, our study has outlined a model of divine love (ch. 2) which complicates a straightforward theology of mission. In his poietic giving God gives us what we lack and what we really need. If we are to love our neighbor according to this model of divine love, we are not to look at our own gifts but at our neighbor's needs. True and genuine giving thus "brackets" the self-interest and the resources of the giver and looks only at the recipient's needs. We should not "colonize" our neighbor through exporting our own goods, but the neighbor's needs are to be considered without any regard to our interests.

Of course, following this "rule of divine love" does not automatically alter any particular concrete case. If I am convinced that papacy or speaking in tongues is the ultimate gift of God to me and that it is also the very thing my neighbor needs, then I will probably give this gift to my neighbor and think that I am not following self-interest, but the rule of divine love. In addition to the rule itself, we probably also need some act of faith, saying to us that we can "bracket" our self-interest in exercising neighborly love and, after doing this, can give genuine gifts. Perhaps we should first exercise *metanoia*, repentance, in order to bracket our self-interest and only after that exercise poietic love.

We will not develop the theocentric aspect of gift exchange any further but refer to our interpretations of the golden rule in chapter 2 and to our discussion of human "disengagement" in chapter 5. It must be said that following God's love is also not a "gift exchange," since in this love we do not give God back anything in exchange. God is rather the initiator of the subsequent interhuman mutual aid or gift exchange. Therefore it is finally only the interhuman form which counts as "gift exchange" in the strict sense. And this sense is characterized, as we said above, by the inherent freedom of the gift. God's preceding action can motivate us, but it does not determine our love. There is no automatism of love.

The exchange of gifts is a formal or methodological concept of ecumenical theology. Some material issues of ecumenism also appear in a different light when they are looked at from the giver-oriented perspective. Already in the introduction we mentioned two examples: infant baptism and the Orthodox concept of synergy. We remarked that in these cases the inherent freedom found in the recipient is only visible from the giver-oriented perspective, whereas the receiver-oriented view is concerned with minimizing the recipient's activity. We merely identified this phenomenon. Now we must ask: can we, on the basis of our study, explain this phenomenon any further?

Before attempting an explanation, we can observe that at several points our theology of giving has yielded similar results. Concerning forgiveness (ch. 3), human freedom and even initiative is required in an astonishing quantity: we are required to forgive before God forgives. Concerning the imitation of Christ and Christian spirituality (ch. 5), we are not only called to follow and learn through a model, but we must also learn not to covet what our models have and to disengage ourselves toward the inner freedom of the Christian. Sacrifice (ch. 4) is a fascinating but difficult case: on the one hand, we should replace sacrifice by mercy. On the other hand, the Augustinian grammar of sacrifice presupposes that humans offer something to God. Even when Luther criticizes this anthropocentrism, he keeps the idea of "spiritual sacrifice" in which humans exercise an active service while keeping their inner freedom. Concerning the Eucharistic Prayer (ch. 4), the giver-oriented perspective explains in what sense the emphasis on the gift does not abandon the dialogical character of the liturgy, but on the contrary confirms it and affirms *eucharistein*, thanksgiving.

Our giver-oriented perspective has thus highlighted the moment of human freedom in many theological texts and contexts. Given the anti-Pelagian character of Western theology, this is a somewhat unusual result and may raise doubts. It has not been our aim to revise any of the doctrinal positions of classical theology. We have only argued that when they are looked in terms of a "theology of giving," they reveal more of human freedom than the usual receiver-oriented perspective has done. An emphasis on giving and the gift preserves the inherent freedom of human reception. A gift cannot be received mechanically, automatically, or without any response. If it were, we would not speak of giving and receiving, but simply of putting something somewhere, as we said in the Introduction.

There is indeed a small paradox involved: a focus on the receivers minimizes their activity, but when the focus is transferred to the giver, receivers begin to show themselves as living and free partners. When God gives something to us, the theocentric perspective allows us to be more free, whereas the anthropocentric perspective minimizes our freedom. Why is this the case? The first explanation of this paradox has already been given by the very concept of the gift: in order to be a gift, some freedom of both the giver and the recipient must be presupposed. They need not be theologically presupposed, but only conceptually: this is how we use the words "to give" and "gift."

But why does this inherent freedom not show itself in a similar manner when we focus on the recipient? We need a second and deeper explanation: The anthropocentric perspective often does not preserve the mode of the gift but instead lapses into other concepts which lack this mode. In the concept of infused grace, for example, salvation comes like a physical substance from God to us. It is not a physical substance, but it is conceptualized in terms of physical movement. In the effective mode of "infused grace," grace thus resembles a substance which is put into a container. The container is needed in the process of infusion, not in any mode of personal involvement, but as a mere physical object. Other "effective" ways of speaking of grace have similar physicalist underpinnings: they mutate or affect the receiver in some physical but impersonal way. The reception of effective grace happens without an idea of response and therefore makes the receiver an impersonal object. In this sense the mode of the gift is lost.

Another receiver-oriented conceptual figure is that of forensic judgment. In the forensic modes of amnesty, rehabilitation, or declaration, the one who becomes judged is not directly involved in the forensic act, but remains its passive object. Thus the receiver also in these modes becomes synonymous with an inanimate object. In principle, a judge can rehabilitate dead persons or declare that this inanimate thing is no longer what it used to be, for instance that it is no longer someone's property. In this way, the forensic mode of speech also differs dramatically from the mode of giving and response.

Human reception is thus easily downplayed in both a physicalist and a forensic use of language. In both of these prominent Western theological dialects, a problematic objectification of the receiver takes place. The described slide toward impersonal linguistic usages may also have something to do with the broader everyday semantics of receiving: whereas "giver" normally needs to be a person, a "receiver" can be an inanimate thing, for instance a container or an instrument. We have not, however, highlighted this point, but instead claimed that Western theology is so conditioned by its anti-Pelagian attitude that theologians are a priori skeptical about the freedom of the recipient and therefore favor physicalist and forensic conceptualizations.

The second explanation thus says that a receiver-oriented view has a strong tendency to replace the interplay of giving and receiving the gift with radically different conceptual figures. In particular, the forensic and effective figures do not preserve the giver-receiver discourse but very easily treat the receivers as inanimate objects. Strictly speaking, forensic and effective relationships are neither "giver-oriented" nor "receiver-oriented," since, as a result of objectification, they abolish the underlying relationship among the giver, the gift, and the receiver. But for reasons of simplicity, we have referred to the Western anthropocentrism as a "receiver-oriented" view.

Of course our explanation does not mean that we would embrace Pelagianism. Our interpretations claim only that through the giver-oriented optic we have a possibility to approach difficult but classically orthodox topics which seem to provoke quasi-Pelagian results: What is our initiative in forgiveness? Why does the sacrament of baptism need faith and response? What is Christian freedom? We can answer or at least approach these non-Pelagian questions if we adopt a giver-oriented perspective with its view of the inherent freedom implied by the gift.

Receiving, Giving, and Sharing in the Church

Today's ecumenical theology is often dominated by ecclesiology. My approach has not, however, discussed the church thematically. In some sense this is no accident, since I believe that the first 1,500 years of Christianity did quite right in concentrating on other theological topics. Ecclesiology is a latecomer in theology, both historically and dogmatically. Jesus did not preach about the nature and purpose of the church. Christianity may learn more about itself and its communal structure when it does not focus on itself but on God and the world.[3]

But since ecumenical theology is finally about the unity of the church, some ecclesiological reflection is both necessary and fitting in this last section of our study. At present, theological reflection on the church is overwhelmingly done in terms of an "ecclesiology of communion." This concept, as developed by famous ecumenists like Yves Congar, John Zizioulas, and Jean-Marie Tillard has been fruitful in dialogues and in important statements on Christian unity.[4] At the same time, we must admit that the "theology of giving" outlined here does not extensively employ an ecclesiology of communion.

This is not because our approach would be critical of an ecclesiology of communion. In order to outline a theologically comprehensive ecclesiology of communion, one should first discuss trinitarian communion and its relationship to the church. But trinitarian relationships are too subtle and complicated to be understood by the rather straightforward notions of giving and receiving. Even if their historical origin lies in the Johannine language of giving and sending (ch. 2), their subsequent doctrinal development has followed its own paths. The trinitarian definitions of the ecumenical councils remain only remotely connected with the everyday ideas of giving which we have tried to apply in this book. Although the trinitarian definitions are highly important, their ecclesiological significance must therefore be discussed elsewhere.

This does not mean, however, that the approach of the present book would have no ecclesiological underpinnings. I think it has, but they are not found in the trinitarian communion in the first place but rather in the model of the church as the body of Christ or as a communion in Christ. Christological ecclesiology was prominent in the early ecumenical movement. Although it has more recently given way to trinitarian reflection, as a central biblical paradigm the view of the church as the body of Christ is certainly not absent from today's ecumenism. It has recently been employed to some extent in the Princeton Statement *In One Body Through the Cross*.

---

[3] Hans Küng, *The Church* (London: Burns & Oates, 1969) has remained a standard presentation of historical issues and their interpretation.

[4] John Zizioulas, *Being as Communion* (London: Darton, 1985); J.-M.R. Tillard, *Church of Churches: The Ecclesiology of Communion* (Collegeville: Liturgical Press, 1992); Risto Saarinen, "The Concept of Communion in Ecumenical Dialogues," in *The Church as Communion*, ed. Heinrich Holze (Geneva: Lutheran World Federation 1997) 287–316.

The Princeton Statement describes our communion in Christ as the gift of unity that already exists. At the same time, our ecumenical activity should be concerned with the structural form of this communion. How this form is to be understood depends on theological convictions about the church as itself Christ's body.[5] Applying this starting-point, we may say that our study has worked out a specific theological conviction. According to it, Christ's biblical giving and self-giving are models and paradigms of human love and reconciliation (chs. 2, 4). In the sacrament, Christ is both the giver and the gift (ch. 4). God's word gives us Christ and as members of the church we are members of Christ's body and share in communion with him.

A more specific ecclesiology of communion in Christ becomes visible in the figure of poietic love (ch. 2) and especially in the life-forms of struggle, care, and disengagement that together characterize the imitation of Christ in the Christian life (ch. 5). We have in chapter 5 treated these three life-forms from the viewpoint of an individual, which is the classical viewpoint of imitation. But the life-forms can as well become applied to communion in Christ: As a community of struggle, *ecclesia militans,* the church is the body of Christ, a holy and eschatologically triumphant place which for the present nevertheless remains under the cross. As a community of care, the church is a hospice and a hospital, in which the sick and needy are healed. As a spiritual community, the church is a *refugium,* a place of asylum and retreat in which we disengage ourselves from the ways of the world and aim at reaching solitude, peace, and spiritual fulfillment. These classical models of the church are also pictures of imitation. As we have seen in chapter 5, they reflect the life of Christians in their competition, care, and recreation. At the same time, they reflect Christ as an example of human life. The ways in which we receive, give, and share in the life of the church are basically given through these Christological pictures of imitation.

We may apply our "giver-oriented" perspective to this ecclesiology. In the church God gives us all good gifts, as Luther explains in his catechisms (ch. 2). We are also called to follow this rule of divine love and become givers to others. If we understand the poietic love, agape, to mean that we give others what they need and lack, we have to see that our gifts to them are not chosen in order to propagate our own favorite goods. Instead, they should be unselfish and free gifts in the

---

[5] *In One Body through the Cross, The Princeton Proposal for Christian Unity*, eds., Carl Braaten and Robert Jenson (Grand Rapids: Eerdmans, 2003) 16–17.

sense that they are given because others need them. At the same time, we are ourselves in need of some gifts and are served by others who observe and satisfy our needs without imposing obligations on us. This circulation of goods is more a sharing than an exchange. It does not follow a logic of exchange in which products are distributed against payments, debts, and counter-gifts. Sharing remains free and uninterested. It does not aim at a capitalist accumulation of gifts in which everyone will get everything in the long run. It is rather a service in which our daily bread is given us today.

This picture of poietic love is outlined with the help of christology. It is also an ecclesiology of communion which portrays the church as a community of mutual help, aspiration, and peace. These three life-forms imitate Christ, but they also sustain a community. This brief outline still remains far from being a proper ecclesiology. Imitation only sustains the community, but does not constitute it. The constitutive role of word and sacraments as well as the creative and pneumatic work of the trinitarian God should be included before we could really speak of an ecclesiology.

We are thus concerned with an image of the church rather than with the underlying nature and purpose of the church. Therefore, our modest picture of the church as the body of Christ is not a concrete ecumenical program. It may nevertheless contain some concrete proposals for today's ecumenical work. The Princeton Proposal impatiently sets forth structural and institutional changes.[6] Our study will consciously keep its proposals modest, since its main aim has been theological rather than practical and since its ecclesiology remains exemplary. But something can be said.

First, our view of ecumenical sharing argues that everybody does not need to be everything and that ecumenical sharing does not need to become a massive and cumulative exchange in which identities would in the long run be completely lost. This argument is compatible with "reconciled diversity" and "differentiated consensus," that is, ecumenical strategies that allow for some differences within a negotiable and definable unity.[7] We will not, however, define these strategies any closer in this book nor discuss their relationship to more ambitious models, such as visible or organic unity. Perhaps we can add only that whereas "organic unity" consciously applies the Pauline

---

[6] *In One Body*, 17.

[7] For these and other strategies, see e.g., Harding Meyer, *That All May Be One: Perceptions and Models of Ecumenicity* (Grand Rapids: Eerdmans, 1999).

picture of sharing in one body, "visible unity" must be defined in more detail if it is to avoid the problems of cumulative omnipotence described above.

Second, we have consciously brought the notions of *metanoia*, conversion or repentance, and disengagement or inner freedom into our discussion. They point toward spiritual ecumenism and attempt to some extent to describe its nature. Spiritual ecumenism is not an item which could be added on the top of an academic theological dialogue, but it grows organically and conceptually from the theological themes of forgiveness and reconciliation, sacrifice and thanksgiving, imitation and disengagement. Through employing these notions, we have given some conceptual shape to spiritual ecumenism.

Third, our giver-oriented approach emphasizes freedom. This freedom does not, however, point towards relativism or pluralism. It rather points towards preferentialism,[8] a view in which one sticks to one's own tradition while admitting that other traditions can appear as plausible alternatives. Such preferentialism goes together with serious theological work in which positions are argued for and against, but it also goes together with respect for and an acknowledgement of many positions which we cannot fully comprehend, since we do not possess a perspective of omniscience. We may prefer our own tradition, share it with others, and let them share their tradition with us. In many cases, an exchange of gifts takes place as a result, but not necessarily.

In sum, ecumenical sharing is the important thing to which we are called in applying the Pauline picture of body and members. In this way ecumenists can recommend a considerate and respectful preferentialism. We need not be everything nor relativize everything, but we can share our traditions with each other and still affirm and even prefer them. In this sense, new institutional solutions are perhaps not so urgent as many ecumenists claim them to be. We are to be patient with what has been given to us. In this limited sense, there is an element of conservatism or at least patience present in the notion of giving.

We have seen in many different cases that the conceptual shape of "giving" and "the gift" presupposes a significant degree of freedom. When theological issues are discussed in terms of giving and the gift, the inherent freedom implied by this discourse simply must be admit-

---

[8] Preferentialism is not a received ecumenical strategy, but serves here only as a brief illustration. My description of it employs some concepts of Nicholas Rescher, *Pluralism: Against the Demand for Consensus* (Oxford: Clarendon Press, 1993) and William A. Christian, *Doctrines of Religious Communities* (New Haven: Yale University Press, 1987).

ted and accounted for. If it immediately becomes transformed into forensic, effective or some other objectifying language, we loose a central moment of the gift. The giver-oriented perspective attempted in this book wants to preserve the freedom of the gift. Without being Pelagian and yet avoiding the reduction of personal recipients to inanimate objects, the giver-oriented perspective allows us to see theological issues in a new light. We have attempted here to show how they look in this light.

Index